CW01650487

THE BOOK OF

# DRESSINGS & MARINADES

JANICE MURFITT

Photographed by
PAUL GRATER

TED SMART

Specially produced for Ted Smart,
Guardian House, Borough Road,
Godalming, Surrey GU7 2AE.

This book was created by Merehurst Limited,
Ferry House, 51/57 Lacy Road, Putney, London SW15 1PR

©Salamander Books Ltd., 1989

ISBN: 1 85613 155 6

All rights reserved. No part of this publication may be reproduced, stored in a retrieval system, or transmitted in any form or by any means, electronic, mechanical, photocopying, recording, or otherwise, without the prior written permission of the copyright owner.

Commissioned and directed by Merehurst Limited
Managing Editor: Felicity Jackson
Editor: Beverly LeBlanc
Designer: Roger Daniels
Home Economist: Janice Murfitt
Photographer: Paul Grater
Typeset by Angel Graphics
Colour origination by Magnum Graphics Limited
Printed in Belgium by Proost International Book Production, Turnhout

ACKNOWLEDGEMENTS

The publishers would like to thank the following for their help and advice:
The Covent Garden General Store, 111 Long Acre, Covent Garden, London WC2E 9NT
David Mellor, 26 James Street, Covent Garden, London WC2E 8PA, 4 Sloane Square, London SW1W 8EE and 66 King Street, Manchester M2 4NP.
Neal Street East, the Oriental specialist, 5 Neal Street, Covent Garden, London WC2.

**Notes:**
All spoon measurements are equal.
1 teaspoon = 5 ml spoon.
1 tablespoon = 15 ml spoon.

# CONTENTS

# INTRODUCTION

Dressings are a mixture of aromatic ingredients, subtly blended together as an accompaniment to enhance all kinds of fish, meat, vegetable and mixed salads.

Tart and tangy in flavour, they form an uncooked sauce which can transform everyday ingredients into a special occasion dish.

Different salads require different kinds of dressings – varying in consistency, texture, flavour and colour – and to make it easy to find the dressing you want, the dressings are divided into chapters, grouping the various types together.

Marinades are similar to salad dressings in that they are used to add flavour, colour and texture, but they are used primarily on foods being grilled, barbecued or roasted. They can also be used as meat tenderisers, coatings for fish, fruit and vegetables, glazes and sauces.

The marinades section of this book includes chapters on marinades for joints and small cuts of meat, poultry, vegetables and fruit, all beautifully illustrated in colour.

# DRESSINGS

Translucent mixtures of oils, vinegars and herbs are always best suited to leaf salads, whereas the thicker, creamier dressings – using yogurt or cream – cling better to the denser ingredients like avocados, artichokes or mixed bean salads.

Soft and cream cheeses form a thicker consistency when blended with other ingredients. These may be used as dips, served with a selection of crisp, fresh vegetables or fruits, or diluted with fruit juices or vinegars to make dressings.

Fruit and vegetable dressings make a welcome change as they may be used to replace the tartness of vinegar and the richness of oils, and blend well with meat, fish, fruit and vegetable salads.

Mayonnaise is a luxury dressing or accompaniment to salads. Egg yolks, oil and flavourings are blended to produce a thick, rich, creamy dressing to mask meat or fish, coat vegetables, or serve with any leaf, meat or fish salads.

**Oil**

This is the most prominent ingredient in many salad dressings; not only is it the most expensive item in most dressings, but it varies greatly in quality, colour, flavour and texture.

The natural choice for many salad dressings is olive oil. Virgin olive oil – the oil collected from the first cold pressing of the olives – is the best. It has a strong flavour and rich colour. However, the flavour is too intense to blend with delicately flavoured ingredients.

Other oils which offer a choice of flavours and colours are all the nut oils – almond, walnut, coconut, hazelnut and groundnut (peanut).

The most subtle-flavoured and light-textured oils are made from seeds – sunflower, sesame and grapeseed.

**Vinegars**

These are used to blend with oils, forming an emulsion and the base

for the dressings, giving added flavour and colour. Available in a wide variety of flavours, the most popular choice for flavour and quality are the wine vinegars. These come as red, white or rosé.

They often have added ingredients, such as peppercorns, herbs or fruit, to give more variety of flavour and colour. All manner of fresh herbs can be added. Cider vinegar is often blended with honey, herbs and fruit and adds interesting flavour to dressings.

**Soft Cheeses, Yogurts and Cream**
These come in a variety of textures, consistencies and flavours. Use low fat soft cheeses, full fat cream cheese, thick Greek or natural yogurts.

Fromage frais, being low in fat, is useful for a low-calorie dressing, Double (thick), single (light) or whipping creams, which produce thick, creamy dressings, are suitable for dips.

**Fruit and Vegetables**
These offer texture, flavour and colour. Grated peel and juice of fruits can be used to replace vinegars, giving a more subtle-flavoured dressing. Puréed fruit or vegetables may replace oils and, blended with soft cheeses or yogurt, give a low-calorie dressing.

**Fresh Herbs**
These are a must with most dressings as they impart natural freshness, colour and flavour. Add a mixture of freshly chopped herbs to dressing just before serving to give the full benefit of the aroma.

**Spices**
These may be used to enhance the flavour of dressings. Saffron, in particular, imparts its wonderful colour and delicate flavour. Mace, allspice, nutmeg and cloves are better selected in the winter months when fresh herbs are not so readily available.

# ALMOND YOGURT DRESSING

| |
|---|
| 45 g (1½ oz/⅓ cup) ground almonds |
| 2 cloves garlic, crushed |
| ¼ teaspoon salt |
| ½ teaspoon black pepper |
| 1 teaspoon grated lime peel |
| 60 ml (2 fl oz/¼ cup) almond oil |
| 6 teaspoons white wine |
| 125 g (4 oz/½ cup) low fat natural yogurt |
| 2 teaspoons chopped fresh lovage |
| 2 teaspoons chopped fresh oregano |
| 2 teaspoons chopped fresh parsley |

Put ground almonds, garlic, salt, pepper, lime peel and almond oil in a bowl and stir together with a wooden spoon until well mixed.

Stir in wine and yogurt and beat together until blended. Cover with plastic wrap and leave in a cool place until required.

Add chopped herbs and stir well. Serve with a grated carrot and celeriac salad, mixed cooked green, broad or French beans or mixed rice and pasta salads which include meat and fish.

*Makes 155 ml (5 fl oz/⅔ cup).*

**Variations:** Replace ground almonds with ground Brazil, pine or pistachio nuts.

## COCONUT LIME DRESSING

| | |
|---|---|
| 60 g (2 oz) creamed coconut |
| 1 teaspoon grated fresh root ginger |
| 2 teaspoons finely grated lime peel |
| 3 teaspoons freshly squeezed lime juice |
| 1 teaspoon clear honey |
| 125 g (4 oz/½ cup) strained Greek yogurt |

Put coconut and 6 teaspoons boiling water in a bowl, stirring until smooth. Leave until cold.

Stir in ginger, lime peel and juice, honey and yogurt until well blended. Cover with plastic wrap and leave in a cool place until required.

Use to toss mixed fresh fruit for a fruit salad, on an onion and potato salad or a grape, pear and cream cheese salad.

*Makes 155 ml (5 fl oz/⅔ cup).*

**Variations:** Replace lime peel and juice with lemon, orange or grapefruit peel and juice.

# EGG & WALNUT DRESSING

| | |
|---|---|
| **2 hard-boiled eggs, peeled and roughly chopped** |
| **1 teaspoon light soft brown sugar** |
| **¼ teaspoon cayenne pepper** |
| **1 teaspoon Dijon mustard** |
| **1 teaspoon dry mustard** |
| **60 ml (2 fl oz/¼ cup) walnut oil** |
| **3 teaspoons cider vinegar** |
| **125 g (4 oz/½ cup) Greek yogurt** |
| **3 teaspoons chopped walnuts** |

Press eggs through a sieve over a bowl using a wooden spoon, or blend in a food processor.

Add sugar, cayenne pepper, mustards and oil and beat until well blended. Stir in vinegar and beat until cloudy and slightly thick. Stir in yogurt and walnuts until well mixed. Cover the dressing with plastic wrap and leave in a cool place until required.

Serve this piquant dressing with all meat and fish dishes, hot or cold. Mix together with cold rice and pasta as a base for a meat, fish or vegetable salad.

*Makes 155 ml (5 fl oz/⅔ cup).*

**Variation:** Add 4 teaspoons chopped fresh mixed herbs and replace walnut oil and walnuts with hazelnut oil and hazelnuts.

## ORANGE & HERB YOGURT

| | |
|---|---|
| 1 teaspoon finely grated orange peel | |
| 6 teaspoons freshly squeezed orange juice | |
| 1 clove garlic, crushed | |
| 60 ml (2 fl oz/¼ cup) sunflower oil | |
| 125 g (4 oz/½ cup) strained Greek yogurt | |
| 2 teaspoons chopped fresh rosemary | |
| 2 teaspoons chopped fresh coriander | |
| 2 teaspoons chopped fresh parsley | |

Put orange peel and juice, garlic and oil in a bowl and beat with wooden spoon until well blended. Stir in yogurt.

Cover with plastic wrap and leave in a cool place until required. Stir in the chopped mixed herbs and serve at once.

Use this light dressing with sliced beetroot, chopped cucumber, potato and cooked vegetable salads and any curried dish.

*Makes 155 ml (5 fl oz/⅔ cup).*

**Variations:** Replace orange peel and juice with lime, lemon or grapefruit peel and juice, or raspberry, strawberry or currant juices.

# PEPPERCORN DRESSING

| | |
|---|---|
| **4 teaspoons hazelnut oil** |
| **1 teaspoon raspberry vinegar** |
| **1 teaspoon pink peppercorns, crushed** |
| **1 teaspoon green peppercorns, crushed** |
| **1 teaspoon caster sugar** |
| **¼ teaspoon salt** |
| **125 g (4 oz/¼ cup) strained Greek yogurt** |

Put oil, vinegar, peppercorns, sugar and salt in a bowl and mix together with a wooden spoon until cloudy and slightly thick.

Stir in yogurt. Cover with plastic wrap and leave the dressing in a cool place until required.

Serve with grilled steak or fish, or use to toss a mixture of apple, nut, celery and seeds or a tomato, olive, onion and mixed red and green peppers (capsicums) salad.

*Makes 155 ml (5 fl oz/⅔ cup).*

**Variations:** Add 4 teaspoons chopped fresh mixed herbs such as parsley, thyme, mint, sage, oregano or marjoram, or 4 teaspoons chopped pickled vegetables such as courgettes (zucchini), onions or cauliflower flowerets.

# TOMATO & OLIVE DRESSING

| | |
|---|---|
| 2 tomatoes, weighing about 125 g (4 oz) | |
| ¼ teaspoon salt | |
| ½ teaspoon black pepper | |
| 1 teaspoon caster sugar | |
| 125 g (4 oz/½ cup) Greek yogurt | |
| 8 black olives, chopped | |
| 3 teaspoons chopped fresh parsley | |
| 3 teaspoons chopped fresh chervil | |

Plunge tomatoes into boiling water for 30 seconds, then pierce skins and peel off. Halve tomatoes and remove seeds.

Press tomatoes through a sieve or place in a food processor fitted with a metal blade. Process tomatoes until puréed.

Stir in salt, pepper, sugar and yogurt until well blended. Cover with plastic wrap and leave in a cool place until required. Add olives and herbs and stir to blend well.

Serve with a celery, apple and potato salad, or a salad of cauliflower and broccoli flowerets mixed with chopped walnuts.

*Makes 155 ml (5 fl oz/⅔ cup).*

# VINAIGRETTE DRESSING

| |
|---|
| 1/4 teaspooon salt |
| 1/2 teaspoon black pepper |
| 1 teaspoon Dijon mustard |
| 1 teaspoon caster sugar |
| 155 ml (5 fl oz/2/3 cup) olive oil |
| 6 teaspoons tarragon vinegar |
| 6 teaspoons white wine vinegar |

Put salt, pepper, mustard, sugar and oil in a bowl and whisk well.

Add tarragon and wine vinegars, whisking until cloudy and slightly thick. Cover with plastic wrap and leave in a cool place until required. This is an all-purpose dressing; use to toss any salad mixtures.

*Makes 155 ml (5 fl oz/2/3 cup).*

**Variations:** For Herbed Dressing: Add 2 teaspoons snipped fresh chives, 2 teaspoons chopped fresh parsley, 2 teaspoons chopped fresh marjoram and 1 crushed clove garlic with the vinegars and mix until well combined.

For Lemon Dressing: Replace sugar with 2 teaspoons clear honey and tarragon vinegar with lemon juice and add 2 teaspoons finely grated lemon peel and 3 teaspoons chopped fresh lemon verbena. Mix well together.

For Garlic Dressing: Add 2 crushed cloves garlic and 3 teaspoons chopped fresh parsley. Mix until thoroughly combined.

# HERBED VERMOUTH DRESSING

| | |
|---|---|
| ¼ teaspoon dry mustard | |
| ¼ teaspoon salt | |
| ½ teaspoon black pepper | |
| ½ teaspoon light soft brown sugar | |
| 140 ml (4½ fl oz/½ cup) grapeseed oil | |
| 6 teaspoons sweet red or dry white vermouth | |
| 2 teaspoons chopped fresh purple basil | |
| 1 teaspoon chopped fresh hyssop | |
| 1 teaspoon chopped fresh dill | |

Place mustard, salt, pepper, sugar and oil in a bowl and whisk together until well blended.

Add vermouth and whisk until cloudy and slightly thick. Cover with plastic wrap and leave in a cool place until required.

Just before using, stir in basil, hyssop and dill. Serve with a mushroom, apple, nut and celery salad, or marinate mushrooms and thin slices or chunks of melon in this dressing for 1-2 hours in a cool place, then serve as a starter.

*Makes 155 ml (5 fl oz/⅔ cup).*

**Variations:** Replace vermouth with elderflower wine and herbs with 4 teaspoons elderflower heads. Alternatively, replace vermouth with mead and substitute 1 teaspoon clear honey for the sugar. Add 3 teaspoons chopped fresh mint instead of the herbs.

# GINGER LIME DRESSING

| |
|---|
| **2 teaspoons grated fresh root ginger** |
| **1 clove garlic, crushed** |
| **¼ teaspoon salt** |
| **½ teaspoon black pepper** |
| **finely grated peel of 1 lime** |
| **2 teaspoons clear honey** |
| **100 ml (3½ fl oz/½ cup) grapeseed oil** |
| **6 teaspoons freshly squeezed lime juice** |
| **3 teaspoons chopped fresh coriander** |

Put ginger, garlic, salt, pepper, lime peel, honey and oil in a bowl and stir together with a wooden spoon until thoroughly combined.

Add lime juice and beat until cloudy and slightly thick. Cover with plastic wrap and leave in a cool place until required.

Just before using, stir in the coriander. Use to serve with a mixed fish, mushroom and pepper (capsicum) salad, or cooked mixed vegetables with slices of chicken and ham.

*Makes 155 ml (5 fl oz/⅔ cup).*

# MINT & RASPBERRY DRESSING

| |
|---|
| **6 teaspoons chopped fresh mint** |
| **3 teaspoons light soft brown sugar** |
| **140 ml (4½ fl oz/½ cup) grapeseed oil** |
| **50 g (2 oz/⅓ cup) raspberries** |
| **6 teaspoons raspberry vinegar** |
| **2 teaspoons pink peppercorns, crushed** |

Put mint, sugar and 3 teaspoons boiling water in a bowl and stir until sugar has dissolved. Leave to cool.

Using a wooden spoon, stir in oil until well blended. Place a sieve over the bowl and, using a wooden spoon, press raspberries through so only the seeds remain in sieve.

Add vinegar and peppercorns and beat until evenly blended. Cover with plastic wrap and leave in a cool place until required.

Serve with any mixed salad ingredients, including artichokes, avocado, lamb, chicken, duck, salmon or trout.

*Makes 155 ml (5 fl oz/⅔ cup).*

**Variations:** Replace raspberries with the same quantity of loganberries, blackberries, strawberries, red-currants or blackcurrants.

# ORANGE & SESAME DRESSING

1 teaspoon tarragon and thyme mustard
¼ teaspoon salt
½ teaspoon black pepper
1 teaspoon finely grated orange peel
140 ml (4½ fl oz/½ cup) sesame seed oil
6 teaspoons freshly squeezed orange juice
3 teaspoons sesame seeds
3 teaspoons chopped fresh tarragon
2 teaspoons chopped fresh thyme

Put mustard, salt, pepper, orange peel and oil in a bowl and whisk together until well blended.

Add orange juice and sesame seeds and whisk until mixture becomes cloudy and slightly thick. Cover with plastic wrap and leave in a cool place.

Just before using, stir in tarragon and thyme.

Serve with bitter leaf salads such as endive, radicchio, watercress and sorrel.

*Makes 155 ml (5 fl oz/⅔ cup).*

**Variations:** Replace the grated orange peel and the juice with either lemon, lime or grapefruit peel and juice.

# SAFFRON & PISTACHIO DRESSING

| |
|---|
| 1 teaspoon saffron strands or good pinch powdered saffron |
| 2 teaspoons clear honey |
| ¼ teaspoon salt |
| ½ teaspoon black pepper |
| 75 ml (2½ fl oz/⅓ cup) almond oil |
| 2 teaspoons orange flower water |
| 6 teaspoons white wine vinegar |
| 3 teaspoons finely chopped pistachio nuts |

Mix together saffron and honey with 3 teaspoons boiling water until well blended. Leave until cold.

Add salt, pepper and almond oil and whisk until evenly mixed. Whisk in orange flower water and vinegar until cloudy and slightly thick. Cover with plastic wrap and leave the dressing in a cool place until ready to use.

Just before using, stir in pistachio nuts. Use to mix with pasta, rice, cabbage or leaf salads.

*Makes 155 ml (5 fl oz/⅔ cup).*

**Variations:** Replace pistachio nuts with pine nuts.

# SHERRY & CHILLI DRESSING

| |
|---|
| 1 shallot, finely chopped |
| 1 teaspoon finely chopped seeded red chilli |
| 1 clove garlic, crushed |
| 1 teaspoon light soft brown sugar |
| ¼ teaspoon salt |
| ½ teaspoon black pepper |
| 140 ml (4½ fl oz/½ cup) olive oil |
| 6 teaspoons sherry vinegar |

Put shallot, chilli, garlic, sugar, salt, pepper and oil in a bowl and mix.

Add sherry vinegar and beat until mixture becomes cloudy and evenly blended. Cover with plastic wrap and leave the dressing in a cool place until required.

Serve with a mixed bean salad, such as kidney, flageolet, haricot or black beans, or hard-boiled eggs, chick peas, mixed salad ingredients and tuna fish.

*Makes 155 ml (5 fl oz/⅔ cup).*

**Variations:** Replace chilli with 4 teaspoons chopped sweet red or yellow pepper (capsicum) for a milder dressing.

# SPICED BITTERS DRESSING

| |
|---|
| **2 teaspoons allspice berries, crushed** |
| **¼ teaspoon salt** |
| **½ teaspoon black pepper** |
| **½ teaspoon Dijon mustard** |
| **1 teaspoon caster sugar** |
| **140 ml (4½ fl oz/½ cup) groundnut oil** |
| **3 teaspoons Angostura bitters** |
| **6 teaspoons red wine vinegar** |

Put allspice, salt, pepper, mustard, sugar and oil in a bowl and whisk together until evenly blended.

Add Angostura bitters and wine vinegar and continue whisking until mixture becomes cloudy and slightly thick. Cover with plastic wrap and leave in a cool place until required.

Serve with a mixed green or leaf salad, such as oakleaf, frisée or cos lettuce, lamb's tongue, endive, chicory or Caesar salad with anchovies, crisp croûtons, garlic and Parmesan cheese.

*Makes 155 ml (5 fl oz/⅔ cup).*

**Variation:** Add 4 teaspoons chopped fresh mixed herbs.

# SUNSET DRESSING

- ¼ teaspoon salt
- ½ teaspoon ground black pepper
- 1 teaspoon Dijon mustard
- 140 ml (4½ fl oz/½ cup) grapeseed oil
- 4 teaspoons Grenadine syrup
- 6 teaspoons blackcurrant wine vinegar
- 6 teaspoons chopped fresh basil

Put salt, pepper, mustard and oil in a bowl and whisk together until well mixed.

Add Grenadine syrup and blackcurrant vinegar and whisk until mixture has blended well together.

Stir in the basil and pour dressing into a glass serving jug or dish. Cover with plastic wrap and leave in a cool place. The dressing will separate into several layers from pale yellow to deep red with herbs suspended in the middle. Stir just before pouring.

Use to pour over mixed salads of all kinds. It is especially good with avocado and orange salad, cold meat and mixed salads or celeriac, carrot and Jerusalem artichokes.

*Makes 155 ml (5 fl oz/⅔ cup).*

**Variation:** Replace blackcurrant vinegar and chopped fresh basil with raspberry vinegar and a few fresh or frozen raspberries.

## SWEET & SOUR DRESSING

- 1 shallot, finely chopped
- 1 clove garlic, crushed
- ¼ teaspoon salt
- ½ teaspoon black pepper
- ½ teaspoon paprika
- 2 teaspoons French mustard
- 4 teaspoons light soft brown sugar
- 1 teaspoon Worcestershire sauce
- 3 teaspoons tomato purée (paste)
- 140 ml (4½ fl oz/½ cup) olive oil
- 75 ml (2½ fl oz/⅓ cup) blackcurrant vinegar
- ¼ yellow pepper (capsicum)
- ¼ red pepper (capsicum)

Put shallot, garlic, salt, pepper, paprika, mustard, sugar, Worcestershire sauce, tomato purée (paste) and oil in a bowl. Beat with a wooden spoon until well blended.

Add vinegar and beat until cloudy and slightly thick. Cover with plastic wrap and leave in a cool place until ready to use.

Place peppers (capsicums) under a hot grill, skin side uppermost, until skin has charred and bubbled. Peel off skins and chop peppers (capsicums) finely, then set aside until cold.

Add peppers (capsicums) to dressing and stir until well blended.

Serve with mixed rice salad or a cabbage, apple and onion salad.

*Makes 155 ml (5 fl oz/⅔ cup).*

# GRAPEFRUIT GINGER DRESSING

**2 teaspoons finely grated grapefruit peel**
**¼ teaspoon salt**
**¼ teaspoon black pepper**
**¼ teaspoon dry mustard**
**140 ml (4½ fl oz/½ cup) almond oil**
**6 teaspoons ginger wine**
**6 teaspoons freshly squeezed grapefruit juice**

Put grapefruit peel, salt, pepper, mustard and oil in a bowl and mix together with a wooden spoon until well blended.

Add ginger wine and grapefruit juice and beat until cloudy and slightly thick. Cover with plastic wrap and leave in a cool place until ready to use. Whisk before serving.

Serve with a red cabbage and apple salad, or beetroot and celery.

*Makes 155 ml (5 fl oz/⅔ cup).*

**Variations:** Substitute orange, lemon or lime peel and juice for the grapefruit. Add 4-5 teaspoons chopped fresh mint or rosemary to give added flavour and colour.

# WALNUT DRESSING

| | |
|---|---|
| 1 teaspoon light soft brown sugar | |
| 1 teaspoon Dijon mustard | |
| ¼ teaspoon salt | |
| ½ teaspoon black pepper | |
| 140 ml (4½ fl oz/½ cup) walnut oil | |
| 6 teaspoons cider vinegar | |
| 3 teaspoons finely chopped walnuts | |
| 3 teaspoons chopped fresh sage | |

Put sugar, mustard, salt, pepper and walnut oil in a bowl. Whisk together until well blended.

Add cider vinegar and whisk until cloudy and slightly thick. Cover with plastic wrap and leave in a cool place until required.

Stir in walnuts and sage and serve with a mixed hot or cold pasta salad of peppers (capsicums), onions, sweetcorn and pasta.

*Makes 155 ml (5 fl oz/⅔ cup).*

**Variations:** Replace the walnut oil and walnuts with groundnut oil and finely chopped peanuts, almond oil and almonds or hazelnut oil and hazelnuts.

# CELERIAC FENNEL DRESSING

- 60 g (2 oz/⅓ cup) grated celeriac
- 3 teaspoons chopped spring onion
- 6 teaspoons chopped fennel bulb
- 3 teaspoons chopped fennel leaves
- ¼ teaspoon salt
- ½ teaspoon black pepper
- ¼ teaspoon dry mustard
- 1 teaspoon clear honey
- 6 teaspoons green peppercorn vinegar
- 155 ml (5 fl oz/⅔ cup) thick sour cream

Put celeriac, spring onion, fennel bulb and leaves, salt, pepper, mustard and honey in a bowl and mix well together using a wooden spoon. Stir in vinegar and sour cream, then stir until well blended.

Cover with plastic wrap and leave in a cool place until required.

Serve with cold meats and fish or with a potato and bacon salad, a mixed three-bean salad or cold pasta.

*Makes about 315 ml (10 fl oz/1¼ cups).*

**Variations:** Replace celeriac with 6 teaspoons grated fresh horseradish or extra strong horseradish sauce.

# CREAMY AUBERGINE DRESSING

| |
|---|
| 1 small aubergine (eggplant), about 315 g (10 oz) |
| 1 clove garlic, crushed |
| 1/4 teaspoon cayenne pepper |
| 1/4 teaspoon salt |
| 1/4 teaspoon dry mustard |
| 155 ml (5 fl oz/2/3 cup) thick sour cream |
| 4 teaspoons chopped fresh coriander or tarragon |

Place aubergine (eggplant) under a hot grill or in a preheated oven at 200C (400F/Gas 6). Cook, turning occasionally, for 15-20 minutes, until skin has charred and flesh is soft. Cool slightly, then peel off skin and place flesh in a food processor fitted with a metal blade; process until puréed. Alternatively, press aubergine (eggplant) through a sieve using a wooden spoon.

Blend in garlic, cayenne pepper, salt, mustard and sour cream until dressing is smooth.

Cover with plastic wrap and leave in a cool place until required. Just before serving, stir in coriander or tarragon.

Use as a mayonnaise to accompany all types of salads.

*Makes about 315 ml (10 fl oz/1 1/4 cups).*

**Note:** This dressing can also be used as a dip with fresh sticks of vegetables. Creamy in texture, it is also good for coating new potatoes, cooked mixed vegetables, hard-boiled eggs and tuna chunks.

# DILL & CUCUMBER DRESSING

| |
|---|
| 5 cm (2 in) piece cucumber |
| 1/4 teaspoon salt |
| 3 teaspoons chopped fresh dill |
| 2 teaspoons snipped fresh chives |
| 1/4 teaspoon paprika |
| 1 teaspoon finely grated orange peel |
| 3 teaspoons orange juice |
| 155 ml (5 fl oz/2/3 cup) thick sour cream |

Peel cucumber, cut into 0.5 cm (1/4 in) dice, then place in a bowl and sprinkle with salt. Leave for 30 minutes in a cool place.

Meanwhile, in a bowl, mix dill, chives, paprika, orange peel and juice and sour cream together. Stir until evenly blended. Cover with plastic wrap and leave in a cool place until required.

Drain cucumber, pat dry on absorbent kitchen paper, then stir into sour cream mixture.

Serve with potato salad or with cold mixed cooked vegetables such as cauliflower, beans, peas and courgettes (zucchini).

*Makes about 155 ml (5 fl oz/2/3 cup).*

**Variation:** Replace the dill with other fresh herbs, such as chopped mint, thyme or basil.

# LENTIL DRESSING

| | |
|---|---|
| 60 g (2 oz/⅓ cup) red lentils | |
| ¼ teaspoon salt | |
| ½ teaspoon black pepper | |
| ¼ teaspoon grated nutmeg | |
| 3 teaspoons snipped fresh chives | |
| 155 ml (5 fl oz/⅔ cup) thick sour cream | |

Put lentils in a saucepan with 315 ml (10 fl oz/1¼ cups) boiling water, cover and simmer for 20 minutes, until all water has been absorbed.

Pass lentils through a fine sieve using a wooden spoon, or place in food processor fitted with a metal blade and process until puréed.

Stir in salt, pepper, nutmeg, chives and sour cream until evenly mixed, or blend in a food processor for a few seconds.

Cover with plastic wrap and leave in cool place until required. Serve with hard-boiled eggs, anchovies and olives, or with cold meats and cold cooked fish.

*Makes about 155 ml (5 fl oz/⅔ cup).*

**Variation:** For a thinner dressing, add freshly squeezed orange juice, or for a sharper flavour use vinegar.

# APPLE & MADEIRA DRESSING

| | |
|---|---|
| **1 cooking apple, about 315 g (10 oz), peeled, cored and grated** |
| **1 teaspoon light soft brown sugar** |
| **90 ml (3 fl oz/⅓ cup) sunflower oil** |
| **60 ml (2 fl oz/¼ cup) Madeira** |

Put apple in a saucepan with 90 ml (3 fl oz/⅓ cup) water and bring to the boil; cook gently until tender.

Press apple through a sieve over a bowl using a wooden spoon, or process in a food processor fitted with a metal blade until puréed. Stir in sugar and leave mixture until cold.

Beat in oil and Madeira until well blended. Cover with plastic wrap and chill until required.

Serve with a cold pork and rice salad, mixed pasta or hot pork, poultry or game birds.

*Makes 250 ml (8 fl oz/1 cup).*

**Variation:** Add 3-4 teaspoons chopped fresh apple mint to the dressing just before serving.

# CHERRY CINNAMON DRESSING

| | |
|---|---|
| 155 g (5 oz/1 cup) sweet cherries, stoned |
| 90 ml (3 fl oz/⅓ cup) rosé wine |
| ¼ teaspoon ground cinnamon |
| 1 teaspoon caster sugar |
| 90 ml (3 fl oz/⅓ cup) grapeseed oil |

Put cherries, wine and cinnamon in a saucepan. Bring to the boil, cover and cook very gently for 2-3 minutes, until cherries are tender.

Press cherries through a sieve into a bowl using a wooden spoon, or using a food processor fitted with a metal blade process cherries until puréed. Leave until cold.

Beat in or process sugar and oil until thick and smooth. Cover with plastic wrap and chill the dressing until required.

Serve with a cold duck, goose or pheasant salad or hot poultry or game. Mix together with apple, celery, nuts and peppers (capsicums) for a salad.

*Makes about 155 ml (5 fl oz/⅔ cup).*

# CRANBERRY ORANGE DRESSING

| | |
|---|---|
| **90 g (3 oz/¾ cup) cranberries** |
| **90 ml (3 fl oz/⅓ cup) freshly squeezed orange juice** |
| **2 teaspoons finely grated orange peel** |
| **3 teaspoons clear honey** |
| **60 ml (2 fl oz/¼ cup) groundnut oil** |
| **½ teaspoon ground cinnamon** |
| **3 teaspoons red wine vinegar** |

Put cranberries and juice in a saucepan. Bring to the boil, cover and cook gently until cranberries are tender.

Press cranberries through a sieve into a bowl using a wooden spoon, or use a food processor fitted with a metal blade and process cranberries until puréed.

Add orange peel, honey, oil and cinnamon, then beat or process until thick and smooth. Stir in vinegar until well blended. Cover with plastic wrap and chill the dressing until required.

Serve as an accompaniment to roast turkey, goose, duck or game birds. Also serve with cold poultry or game salads and pâtés.

*Makes 250 ml (8 fl oz/1 cup).*

## GOOSEBERRY MINT DRESSING

| | |
|---|---|
| 125 g (4 oz/⅔ cup) gooseberries, topped and tailed |
| 6 teaspoons caster sugar |
| 6 teaspoons chopped fresh mint |
| ½ teaspoon grated nutmeg |
| 90 ml (3 fl oz/⅓ cup) olive oil |
| 6 teaspoons fromage frais |

Place gooseberries and 6 teaspoons water in a saucepan over a gentle heat. Bring to the boil, cover and simmer 3-4 minutes, until tender.

Pour gooseberries and cooking liquid into a sieve over a bowl and press through with a wooden spoon.

Stir sugar, mint and nutmeg into gooseberry purée, then leave until completely cold.

Beat oil into purée until evenly blended and thick, then stir in fromage frais until smooth. Cover with plastic wrap and chill the dressing until required.

Serve with grilled mackerel, herring or trout or fish pâtés. Use to toss mixed leaf salads and mixed cabbage, apple, celery and onion salads.

*Makes 250 ml (8 fl oz/1 cup).*

# POMEGRANATE MELON DRESSING

| |
|---|
| 1 pomegranate |
| ½ Ogen or charentais melon |
| 2 teaspoons finely grated lime peel |
| 3 teaspoons freshly squeezed lime juice |
| ½ teaspoon ground mace |
| 3 teaspoons chopped fresh lemon thyme |

Peel pomegranate, remove all seeds and place seeds in a sieve over a bowl. Press the pomegranate juice through with a wooden spoon.

Scoop seeds out of melon, then press melon flesh through sieve with wooden spoon into pomegranate juice. Stir in lime peel and juice, mace and thyme and mix well together. Cover with plastic wrap and chill until required.

Serve with mixed fruit salads, leaf salads and fish dishes.

*Makes 250 ml (8 fl oz/1 cup).*

## TROPICAL DRESSING

| |
|---|
| 1 mango |
| 2 passion fruit |
| 1 teaspoon grated fresh root ginger |
| 90 ml (3 fl oz/⅓ cup) almond oil |
| 6 teaspoons blackcurrant vinegar |
| 3 teaspoons chopped fresh borage |

Peel mango and cut flesh away from stone. Press flesh through a sieve over a bowl using a wooden spoon.

Cut passion fruit into halves, scoop out seeds and flesh. Press through a fine sieve into the mango juice until only the passion fruit seeds remain in the sieve.

Stir in root ginger and oil and beat until thick, then add vinegar and borage. Stir until well blended. Cover with plastic wrap and chill until required.

Serve with mixed fruit salads, curry dishes, poultry and fish.

*Makes about 250 ml (8 fl oz/1 cup).*

# GAZPACHO DRESSING

| | |
|---|---|
| 2 tomatoes, skinned, seeded and chopped | |
| 90 g (3 oz/1 ½ cups) soft breadcrumbs | |
| 60 ml (2 fl oz/¼ cup) sherry vinegar | |
| 90 ml (3 fl oz/⅓ cup) olive oil | |
| 3 teaspoons finely chopped shallots | |
| 3 teaspoons finely chopped red pepper (capsicum) | |
| 3 teaspoons finely chopped green pepper (capsicum) | |
| 5 cm (2 in) piece cucumber, peeled and finely chopped | |
| 2 teaspoons chilli and garlic sauce | |
| ¼ teaspoon salt | |
| ½ teaspoon black pepper | |
| 1 teaspoon Dijon mustard | |

Put chopped tomatoes, breadcrumbs, sherry vinegar and olive oil into a bowl and beat together with a wooden spoon until well blended.

Stir in shallots, peppers (capsicums), cucumber, chilli and garlic sauce, salt, pepper and mustard until well blended. Alternatively, using a food processor fitted with a metal blade, add all the ingredients and process until puréed. Cover with plastic wrap and chill the dressing until required.

Serve with Salad Niçoise with peppers (capsicums), onions, olives, anchovies, beans, eggs and tomatoes, or serve with mixed vegetable or leaf salads.

*Makes 250 ml (8 fl oz/1 cup).*

# GREEN LENTIL DRESSING

| | |
|---|---|
| **60 g (2 oz/⅓ cup) green lentils, soaked overnight** | |
| **½ teaspoon salt** | |
| **½ teaspoon black pepper** | |
| **1 clove garlic** | |
| **3 teaspoons grated onion** | |
| **½ green chilli, seeded and chopped** | |
| **3 teaspoons chopped fresh parsley** | |
| **90 ml (3 fl oz/⅓ cup) hazelnut oil** | |
| **60 g (2 oz/¼ cup) fromage frais** | |

Cook lentils in 315 ml (10 fl oz/1¼ cups) boiling water for 20 minutes, or until all water has been absorbed.

Place lentils, salt, pepper, garlic, onion, chilli, parsley and hazelnut oil in a food processor fitted with a metal blade; process mixture until puréed.

Add fromage frais and process until smooth and creamy. Pour into a bowl, cover with plastic wrap and chill until required. Serve as an accompaniment to vegetarian food or as a dip, or use to toss potato or vegetable salads.

*Makes 250 ml (8 fl oz/1 cup).*

# SWEET PEPPER DRESSING

| | |
|---|---|
| 2 red peppers (capsicums), about 250 g (8 oz) | |
| 1 clove garlic, crushed | |
| 1 teaspoon paprika | |
| ¼ teaspoon salt | |
| ¼ teaspoon black pepper | |
| ½ teaspoon dry mustard | |
| 140 ml (4½ fl oz/½ cup) olive oil | |
| 3 teaspoons raspberry vinegar | |

Preheat a hot grill or oven to 200C (400F/Gas 6). Grill or bake peppers (capsicums) for 10-15 minutes, turning occasionally, until skin is charred and flesh is tender.

Peel off skin and remove stalks and seeds from peppers (capsicums). Put into food processor fitted with a metal blade and process until puréed. Alternatively, press peppers (capsicums) through a sieve using a wooden spoon.

Place garlic, paprika, salt, pepper, mustard and oil in a bowl and mix well together. Add vinegar and pepper (capsicum) purée and beat together until mixture thickens slightly. Cover with plastic wrap and chill until required.

Serve with layered vegetable pâtés or sliced avocado as a starter, or use to toss mixed leaf salads.

*Makes 250 ml (8 fl oz/1 cup).*

# TWIN BEAN DRESSINGS

RED BEAN DRESSING:
60 g (2 oz/⅓ cup) cooked red kidney beans, well drained and rinsed if canned
1 clove garlic, crushed
60 ml (2 fl oz/¼ cup) sunflower oil
3 teaspoons blackcurrant vinegar
¼ teaspoon salt
¼ teaspoon black pepper

WHITE BEAN DRESSING:
60 g (2 oz/⅓ cup) cooked white kidney beans, well drained and rinsed if canned
60 ml (2 fl oz/¼ cup) sunflower oil
6 teaspoons fromage frais
¼ teaspoon salt
¼ teaspoon black pepper
1 teaspoon chopped fresh tansy
1 teaspoon chopped fresh caraway
1 teaspoon snipped fresh chives

To make the red bean dressing, put red kidney beans, garlic and oil into food processor fitted with a metal blade; process until puréed.

Add vinegar, salt and pepper and process until mixture is smooth. Pour into a bowl, cover with plastic wrap and chill until required.

To make the white bean dressing, rinse out food processor, then add white kidney beans and oil and process until puréed.

Add fromage frais, salt, pepper and herbs and process until smooth. Pour into a bowl, cover with plastic wrap and chill until required.

Serve as separate creamy dressings, or partially blend together to give a marbled effect.

Serve with hot or cold vegetables, or with vegetarian nut burgers or a nut and mushroom loaf. Alternatively, use as a dip.

*Makes 250 ml (8 fl oz/1 cup).*

# YELLOW TARRAGON DRESSING

| | |
|---|---|
| **2 yellow peppers (capsicums), about 250 g (8 oz)** |
| **1 teaspoon finely grated orange peel** |
| **140 ml (4½ fl oz/½ cup) almond oil** |
| **3 teaspoons tarragon vinegar** |
| **¼ teaspoon salt** |
| **¼ teaspoon black pepper** |
| **1 teaspoon Dijon mustard** |
| **3 teaspoons chopped fresh tarragon** |

Preheat a hot grill or oven to 200C (400F/Gas 6). Grill or bake peppers (capsicums) for 10-15 minutes, turning occasionally, until skin is charred and flesh is tender.

Peel off skins, remove stalks and seeds from peppers (capsicums). Put into food processor fitted with a metal blade and process until puréed. Alternatively, press peppers (capsicums) through a sieve using a wooden spoon.

Put orange peel, oil, vinegar, salt, pepper and mustard into a bowl and mix together with a wooden spoon until cloudy and slightly thick.

Stir in pepper (capsicum) purée and the chopped fresh tarragon and beat until thick. Cover with plastic wrap and chill the dressing until required.

Serve with vine leaves with a lamb and rice stuffing, or try using radicchio, chard and lettuce leaves stuffed with a rice mixture and dressing poured over.

*Makes 250 ml (8 fl oz/1 cup).*

# GREEK DRESSING

- **4 new potatoes, about 125 g (4 oz), cooked**
- **2 cloves garlic, crushed**
- **4 teaspoons ground almonds**
- **140 ml (4½ fl oz/½ cup) almond oil**
- **juice of 1 orange**
- **6 teaspoons white wine vinegar**
- **6 teaspoons chopped fresh mint**

Mash potatoes in a bowl, then add garlic, almonds and oil, beating well with wooden spoon until smooth. Alternatively, use a food processor fitted with a metal blade and process until quite smooth.

Stir in orange juice, vinegar and mint until evenly blended. If dressing is too thick, thin with cold water. Cover with plastic wrap and chill until required.

Serve with fried or grilled fish, fried aubergine (eggplant) slices or with globe artichokes. This dressing can also be served as a dip with a selection of raw vegetables.

*Serves 4.*

# AVOCADO & BACON DRESSING

| | |
|---|---|
| **4 slices streaky bacon, rinded and cooked until crisp** |
| **1 teaspoon spring onion, finely chopped** |
| **1 teaspoon seeded and finely chopped green chilli** |
| **3 teaspoons chopped fresh basil** |
| **1 teaspoon black pepper** |
| **1 avocado** |
| **1 teaspoon lemon juice** |
| **3 teaspoons green peppercorn vinegar** |

Finely chop the bacon in a food processor fitted with a metal blade. Turn into a bowl and add onion, chilli, basil and black pepper. Mix thoroughly. Cover and chill.

Just before serving, peel and stone avocado, and put in food processor with lemon juice and vinegar; process to make a purée. Add mixture in bowl and blend together. Serve immediately as this dressing may discolour on standing.

Serve with cooked asparagus spears, or a celery and green bean salad, or a prawn salad.

*Makes about 250 ml (8 fl oz/1 cup).*

## STAR FRUIT DRESSING

| |
|---|
| 1 star fruit, sliced |
| 60 g (2 oz) raspberries |
| 140 ml (4½ fl oz/½ cup) hazelnut oil |
| 2 teaspoons pink peppercorns, crushed |
| 3 teaspoons chopped fresh lemon thyme |

Put star fruit and raspberries in a food processor fitted with a metal blade. Process for 30 seconds to purée. Place a sieve over a bowl, pour contents from food processor into sieve, press through juices using a wooden spoon, retaining the raspberry pips in the sieve. Discard the pips.

Add hazelnut oil and peppercorns, whisk together until thoroughly blended. Cover with plastic wrap and leave in a cool place until required. Just before using, stir in thyme. Serve as a dressing with a fruit starter, such as grapefruit and orange, or melon, tomato and avocado, or artichokes.

*Makes about 250 ml (8 fl oz/1 cup).*

# MAYONNAISE

| |
|---|
| 2 large egg yolks |
| ½ teapoon Dijon mustard |
| ½ teaspoon salt |
| ¼ teaspoon black pepper |
| ¼ teaspoon cayenne pepper |
| 315 ml (10 fl oz/1 ¼ cups) olive oil |
| 1 teaspoon lemon juice |
| 6-8 teaspoons white wine vinegar |

Have all ingredients at room temperature. Blend egg yolks, mustard, salt and peppers together in a bowl, using a wooden spoon.

Add oil drop by drop, beating well after each addition until the mayonnaise begins to thicken, then slowly increase flow of oil to a steady stream, beating constantly. When all the oil has been added, beat in lemon juice and enough vinegar to give the flavour required. If mayonnaise is too thick, add some boiling water to make it the consistency of thick cream. Store in a clean screw-top jar in refrigerator until required.

*Makes 470 ml (15 fl oz/1¾ cups).*

**Variations:** Using 155 ml (5 fl oz/⅔ cup) mayonnaise make the following variations.

For Garlic Mayonnaise: Add 2 cloves garlic, crushed.

For Lemon or Lime Mayonnaise: Add 2 teaspoons finely grated lemon or lime peel. Replace vinegar with lemon or lime juice.

For Herbed Mayonnaise: Stir in 1-2 teaspoons chopped fresh tarragon, 1 teaspoon chopped fresh chervil, 1 teaspoon chopped fresh marjoram, 1 teaspoon chopped fresh parsley and 1 teaspoon snipped fresh chives.

For Green Mayonnaise: Add 30 g (1 oz/¼ cup) mixed chopped fresh basil, watercress and parsley.

# QUICK MAYONNAISE

| | |
|---|---|
| 2 large eggs | |
| ½ teaspoon dry mustard | |
| ½ teaspoon salt | |
| ½ teaspoon black pepper | |
| 315 ml (10 fl oz/1¼ cups) olive oil | |
| 1-2 teaspoons white wine vinegar | |

Have all ingredients at room temperature. Put eggs, mustard, salt and pepper into a food processor fitted with a metal blade or a blender and process until smooth.

Leave machine running and add oil drop by drop until mayonnaise begins to thicken, then slowly increase flow of oil to steady stream. When all the oil has been added, add vinegar. Pour mayonnaise into a clean screw-top jar and keep in refrigerator until required.

*Makes 470 ml (15 fl oz/1¾ cups).*

**Variations:** Using 155 ml (5 fl oz/⅔ cup) mayonnaise make the following variations.

For Curried Mayonnaise: Add 1 teaspoon biryani paste and 3 teaspoons mango chutney.

For Chilli Pimento Mayonnaise: Add 1 teaspoon chopped fresh chilli and 3 teaspoons chopped red pimento.

For Mustard Mayonnaise: Add 1 teaspoon dry mustard and 1 teaspoon Dijon mustard.

# BASIL & TOMATO MAYONNAISE

- 3 tomatoes
- 8 teaspoons finely chopped fresh basil leaves
- 1 clove garlic, crushed
- 3 teaspoons snipped fresh chives
- 1 teaspoon caster sugar
- 155 ml (5 fl oz/⅔ cup) Mayonnaise, see page 46
- 6 teaspoons strained Greek yogurt

Put tomatoes in a bowl, cover with boiling water and leave for 1 minute, then drain and peel. Halve tomatoes and remove seeds.

Finely chop tomatoes, then put in a bowl with basil leaves.

Add garlic, chives and sugar and stir together using a wooden spoon. Stir in mayonnaise and yogurt until all ingredients are evenly blended. Cover with plastic wrap and chill until required.

Use to coat pasta or rice for a salad base. Serve as an accompaniment to lamb or chicken kebabs, or use to toss cooked mixed vegetables.

*Serves 4.*

## CELERIAC ONION MAYONNAISE

- 125 g (4 oz) celeriac, finely grated
- 2 teaspoons grated red onion
- 3 teaspoons chopped fresh mint
- 1/4 teaspoon cayenne pepper
- 155 ml (5 fl oz/2/3 cup) Mayonnaise, see page 46
- 6 teaspoons fromage frais

Put celeriac, onion, mint and pepper in a bowl and mix well together, using a wooden spoon.

Stir in mayonnaise and fromage frais until all ingredients are well blended. Cover with plastic wrap and chill until required.

Serve with a mixed bean salad, artichoke and mushroom or orange, asparagus and avocado salad.

*Serves 4.*

# COCKTAIL DRESSING

- 1 teaspoon grated onion
- ¼ teaspoon cayenne pepper
- ½ teaspoon anchovy paste
- ½ teaspoon Tabasco sauce
- 6 teaspoons tomato purée (paste)
- 6 teaspoons olive oil
- 2 teaspoons white wine vinegar
- 155 ml (5 fl oz/⅔ cup) Mayonnaise, see page 46
- 2 teaspoons chopped fresh chervil
- 2 teaspoons chopped fresh parsley
- 2 teaspoons chopped fresh dill
- 60 ml (2 fl oz/¼ cup) whipping cream

Put grated onion, cayenne pepper, anchovy paste, Tabasco sauce, tomato purée (paste), oil and vinegar in a bowl and stir well until all the ingredients are thoroughly blended together.

Stir in mayonnaise and herbs until well mixed. Whip cream until thick, then fold into mayonnaise mixture until smooth and evenly blended. Cover with plastic wrap and chill until required.

Use this dressing for making seafood cocktails or as an accompaniment to salmon, trout, crab or lobster salads.

*Serves 4.*

# FENNEL MAYONNAISE

| |
|---|
| 6 cardamom pods |
| 4 teaspoons finely chopped fennel bulb |
| 4 teaspoons chopped fresh fennel leaves |
| 1 teaspoon finely grated orange peel |
| 6 teaspoons freshly squeezed orange juice |
| 1 teaspoon caster sugar |
| 155 ml (5 fl oz/⅔ cup) Mayonnaise, see page 46 |
| 6 teaspoons fromage frais |

Split open cardamom pods, then place seeds in bowl and crush with a wooden spoon. Add fennel bulb and leaves, orange peel and juice and the caster sugar.

Mix ingredients together until well blended. Stir in mayonnaise and fromage frais until evenly mixed. Cover with plastic wrap and chill until required.

Serve with any mixed leaf salads, a red and white cabbage and apple coleslaw and all kinds of egg, meat, fish or pasta salads.

*Serves 4.*

# ITALIAN MAYONNAISE

| |
|---|
| 1 pimento, chopped |
| 3 teaspoons chopped dill cucumber |
| 3 teaspoons chopped pickled onions |
| 6 teaspoons chopped Italian salami |
| 2 teaspoons anchovy paste |
| 2 teaspoons chopped anchovy fillets |
| 3 teaspoons chopped fresh dill |
| 8 stuffed olives, chopped |
| 155 ml (5 fl oz/⅔ cup) Quick Mayonnaise, see page 47 |

Put pimento, dill cucumber, pickled onions, salami, anchovy paste and fillets, fresh dill and olives in a bowl and mix together well.

Stir in mayonnaise until all ingredients are thoroughly mixed. Cover with plastic wrap and chill.

Use as a base for a pasta or mixed rice salad. Toss potatoes, mixed vegetables, peas and beans in the dressing to coat evenly. Alternatively, serve as an accompaniment to tuna, mackerel or chicken salads.

*Serves 4.*

## PEPPER MAYONNAISE

| |
|---|
| 1 red pepper (capsicum), about 125 g (4 oz) |
| 1 teaspoon chilli and garlic sauce |
| ½ teaspoon Tabasco sauce |
| ½ teaspoon paprika |
| 4 teaspoons chopped fresh oregano |
| 155 ml (5 fl oz/⅔ cup) Quick Mayonnaise, see page 47 |

Preheat a hot grill. Place red pepper (capsicum) on grill rack and grill, turning occasionally, until skin has charred and flesh is tender. Peel off skin, remove seeds and stalk and chop pepper (capsicum) finely. Leave until cold.

Put chopped pepper (capsicum), chilli and garlic sauce, Tabasco sauce, paprika and oregano in a bowl and stir with a wooden spoon until well mixed. Add mayonnaise and stir until all ingredients are evenly blended. Cover with plastic wrap and chill until required.

Use this dressing with moulded rice salads, mixed pasta salads and all sorts of cooked mixed vegetable and potato salads.

*Serves 4.*

**Variations:** For Yellow Pepper Mayonnaise: Replace the red pepper (capsicum) with a yellow pepper (capsicum).

For Green Pepper Mayonnaise: Replace the red pepper (capsicum) with a green pepper (capsicum) and add 2 teaspoons green peppercorns and 1 teaspoon caster sugar.

# TARTARE MAYONNAISE

| |
|---|
| 155 ml (5 fl oz/⅔ cup) Mayonnaise or Quick Mayonnaise, see pages 46 and 47 |
| 6 teaspoons capers, well drained |
| 5 teaspoons chopped gherkins |
| 2 teaspoons chopped fresh tarragon |
| 2 teaspoons chopped fresh parsley |
| 2 teaspoons chopped fresh chervil |
| 2 teaspoons green peppercorns, crushed |
| 6 teaspoons whipping cream |

Put mayonnaise, capers, gherkins, tarragon, parsley, chervil and peppercorns in a bowl and mix together using a wooden spoon until all ingredients are well blended.

Whip cream until thick, then add to mayonnaise mixture and fold in gently until smooth and evenly blended. Cover with plastic wrap and chill until required.

Serve this dressing with all kinds of grilled or fried fish, or use as an accompaniment to cold cooked meat or fish salads.

*Serves 4.*

**Variation:** Replace capers and gherkins with sweet pickled vegetables or piccalilli pickle.

# WALNUT MAYONNAISE

| | |
|---|---|
| 155 ml (5 fl oz/⅔ cup) Mayonnaise, see page 46 | |
| 6 teaspoons finely chopped walnuts | |
| 3 teaspoons chopped fresh rosemary | |
| 1 teaspoon clear honey | |
| 1 teaspoon finely grated orange peel | |
| 6 teaspoons fromage frais | |

Make mayonnaise, replacing olive oil with walnut oil.

Put walnuts, rosemary, honey and orange peel in a bowl and mix together with a wooden spoon until well blended.

Stir in mayonnaise and fromage frais until all ingredients are well blended. Cover with plastic wrap and chill until required.

Use to toss a potato, bacon and sweetcorn salad, hot or cold pasta, or as an accompaniment to cold chicken, turkey or duck.

*Serves 4.*

**Variations:** For Peanut Mayonnaise: Replace walnut oil and walnuts with groundnut oil and finely chopped peanuts.

For Hazelnut Mayonnaise: Replace walnut oil and walnuts with hazelnut oil and finely chopped hazelnuts.

For Almond Mayonnaise: Replace walnut oil and walnuts with almond oil and finely chopped almonds.

# BLUE CHEESE DRESSING

| |
|---|
| **½ teaspoon French mustard** |
| **½ teaspoon black pepper** |
| **1 teaspoon caster sugar** |
| **6 teaspoons hazelnut oil** |
| **1 teaspoon tarragon vinegar** |
| **60 g (2 oz/⅓ cup) Blue d'Auvergne cheese, grated** |
| **90 ml (3 fl oz/⅓ cup) whipping cream** |

Place mustard, pepper, sugar and oil in a bowl and beat together with a wooden spoon. Stir in vinegar and cheese, stirring until well blended.

Whip cream until thick, then add to cheese mixture and fold in until evenly blended. Cover with plastic wrap and leave in refrigerator until required.

Serve with egg, potato and fish salads or a rice and pasta salad.

*Makes 155 ml (5 fl oz/⅔ cup).*

# CHICK PEA DIP

| |
|---|
| 185 g (6 oz/1¼ cups) cooked chick peas, well drained and rinsed if canned |
| 2 cloves garlic, crushed |
| ½ teaspoon salt |
| ½ teaspoon ground black pepper |
| 140 ml (4½ fl oz/½ cup) sesame seed oil |
| 8 teaspoons tahini (sesame seed paste) |
| 2 teaspoons orange juice |
| 90 g (3 oz/⅓ cup) fromage frais |

Press chick peas through a sieve using a wooden spoon to make a purée, or process chick peas in a food processor fitted with a metal blade until puréed.

Stir in garlic, salt and pepper. Add oil drop by drop, beating well, or, if using food processor, into chick pea purée until all oil has been incorporated.

Add tahini, orange juice and fromage frais, blending together well. Cover with plastic wrap and place in refrigerator until required.

Serve in a bowl surrounded by small sticks of carrot, celery, red, green and yellow peppers (capsicums), courgette (zucchini) and cucumber.

*Makes 315 ml (10 fl oz/1¼ cups).*

**Variation:** To make into a dressing, add more orange juice or fromage frais until the dressing is of the consistency required.

# CURRIED PRAWN DIP

- 1 teaspoon tandoori paste
- 1 teaspoon grated onion
- 1 teaspoon grated fresh root ginger
- 1 teaspoon finely grated lemon peel
- 3 teaspoons freshly squeezed lemon juice
- 60 ml (2 fl oz/¼ cup) sunflower oil
- 185 g (6 oz/¾ cup) low fat soft cheese
- 3 teaspoons chopped fresh coriander
- 2 teaspoons curry plant leaves
- 125 g (4 oz/⅔ cup) peeled cooked prawns, chopped

Place tandoori paste, onion, ginger, lemon peel and juice in a bowl and mix together with a wooden spoon.

Beat in oil a little at a time until well blended, then add cheese and beat until smooth.

Stir in herbs and prawns. Cover with plastic wrap and chill until ready to serve.

Serve with biscuits, bread sticks, poppadoms or mixed vegetable sticks. Mix with most salad ingredients to turn them into a curry-flavoured side dish which goes well with chicken or ham and also mixed vegetables.

*Makes 315 ml (10 fl oz/1¼ cups).*

**Variations:** Replace prawns with 4 roughly chopped artichoke hearts. For a thinner dressing, add enough natural yogurt to make desired consistency.

# MUSHROOM DIP

- 60 g (2 oz/¼ cup) unsalted butter
- 185 g (6 oz) button mushrooms, roughly chopped
- ¼ teaspoon Tabasco sauce
- ¼ teaspoon salt
- ½ teaspoon black pepper
- 6 teaspoons chopped fresh spring onions
- 1 teaspoon finely grated lime peel
- 2 teaspoons freshly squeezed lime juice
- 90 g (3 oz/⅓ cup) full fat soft cheese
- 4 teaspoons chopped fresh chervil
- chervil sprigs, and lime slices, to garnish

Melt butter in a saucepan, add mushrooms and fry for 1 minute.

Place mushrooms, Tabasco sauce, salt, pepper and spring onions in a food processor fitted with a metal blade and process until puréed. Add lime peel, juice, cheese and chervil and process until well blended and smooth. Cover with plastic wrap and chill until ready to serve.

Serve in a dish garnished and surrounded by Melba toast, biscuits or raw salad ingredients, such as radishes, small cauliflower flowerets, courgette (zucchini) sticks, celery and tomatoes. Also serve as a thick dressing with mixed salads.

*Makes 315 ml (10 fl oz/1¼ cups).*

# TARAMASALATA

| |
|---|
| 125 g (4 oz) smoked cod's roe |
| 125 g (4 oz/1 cup) dry breadcrumbs |
| 2 teaspoons lemon juice |
| 1 clove garlic, crushed |
| ½ teaspoon black pepper |
| 90 ml (3 fl oz/⅓ cup) olive oil |
| 90 g (3 oz/⅓ cup) low fat soft cheese |
| 6 black olives and parsley sprigs, to garnish |

Using a sharp knife, cut through cod's roe skin and scrape out all the roe into a food processor fitted with a metal blade. Mix together breadcrumbs and 8 teaspoons cold water and add to food processor with lemon juice, garlic and pepper.

Process for several seconds until mixture is well blended. Alternatively, press cod's roe through a sieve and beat in remaining ingredients, except the garnish.

Add oil drop by drop, beating well or using food processor until all oil has been incorporated.

Beat in cheese until mixture is smooth and creamy, then spoon into a dish. Cover with plastic wrap and chill until required.

Garnish with black olives and parsley sprigs, and serve with Melba toast, biscuits or sticks of fresh vegetables.

*Makes 315 ml (10 fl oz/1¼ cups).*

**Variation:** To serve as a thinner dressing, add enough natural yogurt to make the consistency required and serve with avocados or asparagus spears.

# EGG & MUSTARD DRESSING

| | |
|---|
| 2 hard-boiled egg yolks, sieved |
| 1 egg yolk, raw |
| 2 teaspoons dry mustard |
| 6 teaspoons olive oil |
| 1 teaspoon Worcestershire sauce |
| 1 teaspoon white wine vinegar |
| 2 spring onions, finely chopped |
| 155 ml (5 fl oz/⅔ cup) whipping cream |

Put hard-boiled and raw egg yolks and mustard in a bowl and beat together with a wooden spoon.

Beat in oil drop by drop until all oil is incorporated and mixture is smooth and creamy. Stir in Worcestershire sauce, vinegar and spring onions.

Whip cream until thick, then add to egg mixture and fold in gently until mixture is well blended. Cover with plastic wrap and chill until ready to serve.

Serve as an accompaniment to cold beef, pork or chicken salads or use as a substitute for mayonnaise when making egg mayonnaise salad.

*Makes 250 ml (8 fl oz/1 cup).*

**Variations:** For Lemon Mustard Dressing: Replace vinegar with lemon juice and add 1 teaspoon finely grated lemon peel, 1 teaspoon clear honey and 3 teaspoons chopped fresh herbs. Mix in well before adding cream.

# PINK CREAM DRESSING

- 6 teaspoons grated beetroot
- 6 teaspoons grated dessert apple
- 2 teaspoons grated onion
- 1 clove garlic, crushed
- ½ teaspoon ground mace
- ½ teaspoon black pepper
- ¼ teaspoon salt
- 1 teaspoon caster sugar
- 155 ml (5 fl oz/⅔ cup) whipping cream

Place beetroot, apple, onion, garlic, mace, pepper, salt and sugar in a bowl and mix well together using a wooden spoon.

Whip cream until thick, then add to the beetroot and apple mixture and fold in very carefully until evenly blended.

Spoon into a serving dish and serve as an alternative to mayonnaise. Stir before serving as the beetroot liquid separates during standing. This dressing goes especially well with fish salads, rollmop herrings, tuna and mackerel.

*Makes 250 ml (8 fl oz/1 cup).*

# SMOKED SEAFOOD DRESSING

- 2 smoked trout fillets, about 125 g/4 oz, skinned
- 2 teaspoons finely grated lime peel
- 6 teaspoons freshly squeezed lime juice
- 155 ml (5 fl oz/⅔ cup) single (light) cream
- 3 teaspoons snipped fresh chives
- 6 teaspoons chopped fresh watercress
- ¼ teaspoon cayenne pepper
- watercress sprigs and lime wedges, to garnish

Place trout in a food processor fitted with a metal blade, add lime peel and juice and process until smooth.

Add single (light) cream and process again until well blended. Stir in chives, watercress and cayenne. Place in a serving dish and garnish with watercress and lime wedges.

Serve with any seafood salad or with grilled fish. This also makes a good accompaniment to a mixed vegetable or leaf salad

*Makes 250 ml (8 fl oz/1 cup).*

**Variation:** Replace smoked trout fillets with either smoked salmon or mackerel fillets.

# MARINADES

Marinades are capable of changing the appearance, flavour and texture of all types of ingredients. They can also act as a seal – particularly for cuts of meat, preventing moisture escaping during cooking.

The marinades in this book fall into 3 main categories – liquid marinades, dry marinades and pastes, and glazes.

**Liquid Marinades**

Based on a mixture of oils, wine vinegars, herbs and seasonings or fruit juices and grated peel, these are ideal for immersing meat, fish, poultry, game and vegetables to impart flavour and add moisture. The marinade protects the food while it is being cooked over a barbecue, grill or in the oven.

Food may be left for several hours to marinate at room temperature or 24-48 hours in the refrigerator (depending on the food and how hot the weather is). Use these marinades for basting during cooking, and any leftover can be made into quick sauces.

**Dry Marinades and Pastes**

These are simply a blend of mixed dried herbs or spices in the form of leaves, berries, seeds and pods. When crushed in a pestle and mortar, this mixture produces an intense blend of dry ingredients, and with the addition of salt, pepper or sugar, determines the sharpness or sweetness of the mixture required. Rubbed into the surface of meat or fish, or used to toss vegetables to coat evenly, these mixtures impart instant flavour.

To make a paste marinade, mix the above blend of ingredients with fruit peel and juice and garlic or oil to moisten the mixture enough to form a paste. Spread on the surface of meat, fish or poultry to give an even coating, which can then penetrate the food, giving it extra flavour, as well as producing a crispy texture on the surface.

**Glazes**

Quick and easy to prepare, these are simply brushed on to the food's surface before and during cooking. They form a rich glaze, crisp texture and intensely flavoured surface on all foods being cooked. Use thick and clear honey, jellies and preserves, fruit juices and peels and lots of freshly chopped herbs or crushed spices. Try experimenting with different flavour combinations.

**Herbs**

These should be fairly intense in flavour such as fresh or dried bay leaves, rosemary, tarragon, oregano, basil, thyme, sage or marjoram. Use stems of rosemary to thread on to kebabs – they give the food wonderful aromatic flavour. Any mixture of chopped fresh herbs is invaluable to most marinades.

**Oils**

These add moisture and give protection to marinated foods, especially during cooking when they lubricate the food and prevent it from drying out.

**Vinegars and Fruit Juices**

These acid ingredients act as tenderising agents for food. They impart flavour and mix well with oils, producing a full-flavoured marinade. Grated peel from the fruits adds texture and extra flavour, and any leftover marinade may be used as a sauce.

**Spices**

Dried spices in the form of seeds, berries, pods, leaves or bark can be crushed to give a dry marinade. Natural choices are whole cloves, nutmegs, mace, cinnamon sticks, allspice and juniper berries, coriander, mustard, cumin seeds – just to name a few.

Other useful flavoursome ingredients are fresh ginger, garlic, chillies, peppers (capsicums), coconut and curry paste.

# APPLE & ELDERFLOWER PORK

| |
|---|
| **1.25 kg (2½ lb) loin of pork, boned** |
| **4 teaspoons plain flour** |
| MARINADE: |
| **315 ml (10 fl oz/1¼ cups) elderflower wine** |
| **2 heads of elderflowers** |
| **4 teaspoons clear honey** |
| **6 teaspoons almond oil** |
| **3 fresh bay leaves** |
| STUFFING: |
| **250 g (8 oz/2 cups) peeled and chopped cooking apples** |
| **6 teaspoons elderflower wine** |
| **1 teaspoon clear honey** |
| **3 teaspoons snipped fresh chives** |
| **60 g (2 oz/½ cup) white breadcrumbs** |
| GARNISH: |
| **elderflowers** |
| **apple slices dipped in lemon juice** |

Trim any excess fat from meat and remove rind, leaving a thin layer of fat. Score to make a lattice pattern. Mix marinade ingredients together. Immerse pork in marinade. Cover and leave in cool place for 4 hours.

Preheat oven to 190C (375F/Gas 5). To make stuffing, put apples, wine and honey in a pan, bring to boil and cook, stirring, until liquid has been absorbed. Stir in chives and breadcrumbs. Cool.

Remove meat from marinade and pat dry. Spread stuffing over centre, roll up and tie with string. Place in roasting tin, brush with marinade and cook for 1 hour, basting.

Remove meat from tin, stir flour into juices and add remaining marinade and 155 ml (5 fl oz/⅔ cup) water. Bring to boil, and cook for 2 minutes. Strain into a bowl.

Remove string, then cut meat into thin slices. Pour some of the sauce over a serving plate. Arrange pork slices on top and garnish.

*Serves 6.*

# BEEF IN WINE

- 750 g (1½ lb) thick rib braising steak, well trimmed and cubed
- 30 g (1 oz/6 teaspoons) butter
- 185 g (6 oz/2 cups) button mushrooms
- 155 ml (5 fl oz/⅔ cup) beef stock
- 30 g (1 oz/¼ cup) plain flour
- 3 teaspoons tomato purée (paste)
- oregano and winter savory sprigs, to garnish

MARINADE:

- 155 ml (5 fl oz/⅔ cup) red wine
- ½ cucumber, thinly sliced
- 1 red onion, thinly sliced
- 3 teaspoons chopped fresh oregano
- 3 teaspoons chopped fresh winter savory
- 1 clove garlic
- 2 teaspoons brown sugar
- ½ teaspoon salt
- ½ teaspoon black pepper

To make marinade, mix red wine, cucumber, onion, oregano, winter savory, garlic, sugar, salt and pepper together in a casserole. Add meat and stir well. Cover and leave in cool place for 4 hours.

Preheat oven to 180C (350F/Gas 4). Strain marinade into a bowl, remove cucumber slices and place on a plate.

Melt butter in frying pan, add mushrooms, meat, onion and herbs in sieve and fry quickly to brown meat. Add marinade and stock and bring to the boil, then return to casserole.

Cover and cook for 2 hours, until tender. Mix together flour and tomato purée (paste) and stir into casserole to thicken gravy. Add the cucumber slices. Serve garnished with oregano and winter savory.

*Serves* 4-6.

# HORSERADISH STEAK

- 500 g (1 lb) rump steak, cut into thin strips
- 30 g (1 oz/6 teaspoons) butter
- 6 teaspoons sherry
- thyme sprigs, to garnish

MARINADE:

- 4 teaspoons horseradish sauce
- 4 teaspoons strained Greek yogurt
- 2 teaspoons paprika
- 3 teaspoons chopped fresh thyme
- ½ teaspoon salt
- ½ teaspoon black pepper

To make marinade, mix horseradish, yogurt, paprika, thyme, salt and pepper together, stirring until well blended. Add meat and stir to coat evenly. Cover with plastic wrap and leave in a cool place for 1 hour.

Melt butter in frying pan. Remove steak from marinade using a slotted spoon, add to frying pan and cook quickly for 1 minute. Lift strips of steak out and place on a serving dish.

Stir remaining marinade and sherry into pan and bring to the boil, stirring well. Pour over steak on serving dish and garnish with a few sprigs of fresh thyme.

*Serves 4.*

# JUNIPER LAMB

625 g (1¼ lb) loin of lamb, well trimmed and boned
4 teaspoons plain flour
MARINADE:
250 ml (8 fl oz/1 cup) rosé wine
4 teaspoons juniper berries, crushed
2 teaspoons Angostura bitters
2 bay leaves
½ teaspoon salt
½ teaspoon black pepper
STUFFING:
60 g (2 oz/1 cup) fresh white breadcrumbs
60 g (2 oz) pre-soaked dried apricots
2 teaspoons lemon juice
2 teaspoons finely grated lemon peel
2 teaspoons chopped fresh rosemary
GARNISH:
lemon wedges
6 apricots
rosemary sprigs

To make marinade, mix all ingredients together, add lamb and turn to coat evenly. Cover and leave in a cool place for 4 hours or overnight.

Preheat oven to 190C (375F/Gas 5). To make stuffing, process bread, apricots, lemon juice, peel and rosemary in a food processor.

Remove lamb from marinade and pat dry. Spread stuffing over centre of meat, roll up, and tie securely in several places. Place in roasting tin, brush well with marinade and cook for 45-50 minutes, basting with marinade if necessary. Place meat on a serving plate; keep warm.

Stir flour into tin, add remaining marinade and bring to the boil, stirring: add a little water if too thick. Strain into serving bowl.

Remove string from meat, cut meat into thin slices and pour some of sauce over a serving plate. Arrange lamb in centre and garnish.

*Serves 4-6.*

# GAMMON STEAKS

4 gammon steaks, about 625 g (1¼ lb) in weight

MARINADE:

2 teaspoons light soy sauce

3 teaspoons sherry vinegar

6 teaspoons groundnut oil

3 teaspoons clear honey

3 teaspoons chopped fresh rosemary

6 whole cloves

2.5 cm (1 in) stick cinnamon

½ teaspoon ground black pepper

1 cooking apple, peeled and grated

GARNISH:

rosemary sprigs

apple slices

3 teaspoons lemon juice

Soak gammon steaks in cold water for several hours or overnight. Drain and dry on kitchen paper, then place in a shallow dish.

To make marinade, mix soy sauce, vinegar, groundnut oil, honey, rosemary, cloves, cinnamon, pepper and apple together, stirring well.

Pour marinade over gammon steaks and turn to coat evenly. Cover with plastic wrap and leave in a cool place for 1 hour.

Meanwhile, prepare barbecue or preheat grill to hot. Cook gammon for 3-5 minutes, turning once and brushing with extra marinade. Arrange on a warmed serving dish and serve garnished with sprigs of rosemary and the apple slices tossed in lemon juice.

*Serves 4.*

# PEPPERCORN STEAKS

4 fillets of steak, about 500 g (1 lb)
30 g (1 oz/6 teaspoons) butter
3 teaspoons double (thick) cream

MARINADE:
3 teaspoons wholegrain mustard
2 teaspoons green peppercorns, crushed
2 teaspoons pink peppercorns, crushed
3 teaspoons tomato purée (paste)
½ teaspoon salt
2 teaspoons chopped fresh marjoram
2 teaspoons chopped fresh oregano
2 teaspoons chopped fresh basil

GARNISH:
pink and green peppercorns
marjoram and oregano sprigs
basil leaves

To make marinade, mix mustard, the green and pink peppercorns, tomato purée (paste), salt, marjoram, oregano and basil together, stirring until well mixed.

Spread marinade evenly over each fillet steak to coat. Place on a plate, cover with plastic wrap and leave in a cool place for 1 hour or until ready to cook.

Melt butter in frying pan, add fillet steaks and cook quickly to seal surfaces, then turn and cook undersides. Continue cooking for 3-5 minutes according to desired degree of doneness.

Arrange each steak on a warmed serving plate and keep warm. Stir cream into juices in frying pan and bring to the boil.

Pour a little sauce over each steak, then serve garnished with a few pink and green peppercorns, sprigs of oregano and fresh marjoram and basil leaves.

*Serves 4.*

# PEPPERED PORK

| |
|---|
| 4 pork escalopes, about 500g (1 lb) |
| orange slices and ginger mint sprigs, to garnish |
| MARINADE: |
| 1 small yellow pepper (capsicum) |
| 1 small orange pepper (capsicum) |
| 1 clove garlic |
| 4 teaspoons olive oil |
| 2 teaspoons grated orange peel |
| 6 teaspoons freshly squeezed orange juice |
| 2 teaspoons clear honey |
| 6 teaspoons chopped fresh ginger mint |

Peheat oven to 200C (400F/Gas 6). To make marinade, place peppers (capsicums) in an ovenproof dish and bake for 10-15 minutes, until skin has burnt and peels off easily. Cool slightly, then peel and remove stalks and seeds. Place in a food processor fitted with a metal blade and process until smooth. Add garlic, oil, orange peel and juice, honey and chopped ginger mint and process again.

Arrange pork in an ovenproof dish, pour over pepper marinade and turn pork to coat evenly. Cover with plastic wrap and leave in a cool place for 30 minutes.

Cook for 15 minutes, until cooked through. Arrange on a warmed serving dish and garnish with orange slice and mint sprigs.

*Serves 4.*

# POMEGRANATE & LIME LAMB

| | |
|---|---|
| 4 double lamb chops, about 625 g (1 ¼ lb) |
| redcurrant strands and thyme sprigs, to garnish |
| MARINADE: |
| 2 pomegranates, peeled |
| finely grated peel of 1 lime |
| 3 teaspoons freshly squeezed lime juice |
| 3 teaspoons redcurrant jelly |
| 3 teaspoons chopped fresh thyme |
| ¼ teaspoon salt |
| ½ teaspoon black pepper |
| SAUCE: |
| 30 g (1 oz/6 teaspoons) butter |
| 1 small red onion, thinly sliced |
| 15 g (½ oz/6 teaspoons) plain flour |

To make marinade, scrape pomegranate seeds into a sieve over a bowl, reserving a few for garnish. Press remainder through sieve with a wooden spoon to extract juice.

Put 4 teaspoons juice in another bowl with all remaining marinade ingredients.

Put chops in a shallow dish and brush each with marinade to coat evenly. Cover with plastic wrap and leave for 1 hour in a cool place.

Preheat a moderately hot grill. Grill chops for 5-8 minutes on each side, turning once and brushing with marinade. Keep warm.

Melt butter in saucepan, add onion and cook gently for 1-2 minutes, until tender. Stir in flour and cook for 1 minute, stirring, then remove saucepan from heat. Make up remaining pomegranate juice to 250 ml (8 fl oz/1 cup) with juices from the grill pan and water. Stir into saucepan, bring to the boil, stirring, and cook 2 minutes.

Pour a little sauce onto a warmed serving plate, arrange chops on top and garnish with redcurrant strands, reserved seeds and thyme sprigs.

*Serves 4.*

# PORK WITH HERBS

| |
|---|
| **1 pork tenderloin, about 500 g (1 lb), well trimmed** |
| **4 teaspoons plain flour** |
| **4 teaspoons single (light) cream** |
| **oregano sprigs and sage leaves, to garnish** |
| MARINADE: |
| **6 teaspoons olive oil** |
| **3 teaspoons Madeira** |
| **½ teaspoon salt** |
| **½ teaspoon black pepper** |
| **1 teaspoon Dijon wholegrain mustard** |
| **1 teaspoon caster sugar** |
| **3 teaspoons grated onion** |
| **3 teaspoons chopped fresh sage** |
| **3 teaspoons chopped fresh oregano** |

To make marinade, mix oil, Madeira, salt, pepper, mustard, sugar, onion, sage and oregano together, stirring until well blended.

Pour over pork tenderloin in a shallow ovenproof bowl and turn to coat evenly. Cover with plastic wrap and leave in a cool place for 2-3 hours.

Preheat oven to 220C (425F/Gas 7). Cook pork for 15 minutes, basting with marinade if necessary, until tender and cooked through. Place on a plate and keep warm.

Stir flour into remaining marinade in dish and pour into a saucepan. Bring to the boil and cook for 2 minutes, adding a little water if too thick. Remove from heat and stir in cream.

Slice the pork into 1 cm (½ in) slices and pour sauce on to a serving plate. Arrange sliced pork on top and garnish with oregano and sage.

*Serves 4.*

# ROSY ROASTED GAMMON

| |
|---|
| **1.25-1.5 kg (2½-3 lb) piece gammon** |
| **3 teaspoons whole cloves** |
| **2 teaspoons arrowroot** |
| **6 teaspoons redcurrant jelly** |
| **redcurrant strands and oregano sprigs, to garnish** |
| MARINADE: |
| **250 g (8 oz/2 cups) redcurrants** |
| **6 teaspoons light soft brown sugar** |
| **9 teaspoons chopped fresh oregano** |
| **3 teaspoons olive oil** |

Soak gammon joint in cold water for several hours or overnight. Drain and rinse in fresh water, then place in a large saucepan, cover with cold water; bring to the boil.

Cover and simmer for 30 minutes. Remove gammon from saucepan and cool, then peel off rind.

To make marinade, put redcurrants in a sieve over a bowl and press through juice using a wooden spoon. Stir in sugar, oregano and oil and pour into a large bowl. Add gammon joint and turn in marinade to coat. Cover with plastic wrap and leave in a cool place for 1 hour.

Preheat oven to 190C (375F/Gas 5). Using a sharp knife, score fat on gammon into a lattice pattern. Press cloves into each diamond shape and brush with marinade.

Place in a roasting tin and cook for 45-50 minutes, brushing with extra marinade. Cover with foil if the surface becomes too brown.

Place gammon on a serving plate and keep warm. Blend arrowroot and 155 ml (5 fl oz/⅔ cup) water together, add to roasting tin with marinade and stir well to mix with juices. Strain into a saucepan, add redcurrant jelly, then bring to the boil, stirring, and cook for 1 minute. Pour around gammon and garnish.

*Serves 4-6.*

# SAFFRON LAMB CUTLETS

| |
|---|
| 8 lamb cutlets, about 625 g (1¼ lb) |
| 8 sheets filo pastry, thawed if frozen |
| 60 g (2 oz/¼ cup) butter, melted |
| rosemary sprigs and orange slices, to garnish |
| MARINADE: |
| 155 ml (5 fl oz/⅔ cup) thick sour cream |
| 2 teaspoons finely grated orange peel |
| 3 teaspoons freshly squeezed orange juice |
| ½ teaspoon saffron threads or a good pinch powdered saffron |
| 2 teaspoons chopped fresh rosemary |
| ¼ teaspoon salt |
| ¼ teaspoon black pepper |

Trim away any excess fat from each cutlet and strip off fat and skin from each bone above eye of meat, leaving bones clean.

To make marinade, mix sour cream, orange peel and juice, saffron, rosemary, salt and pepper together, stirring until blended.

Place cutlets in a dish and spread marinade over both sides of the meat. Cover with foil and leave in a cool place for 3-4 hours.

Preheat oven to 230C (450F/Gas 8). Cover baking sheet with foil, arrange cutlets a little apart and cook at the top of oven for 5-8 minutes, until marinade has set and chop is tinged with brown. Cool cutlets for 15 minutes.

Brush each piece of filo pastry with butter and fold in half. Wrap each cutlet in pastry, leaving the bone uncovered.

Arrange cutlets on a buttered baking sheet, brush with remaining butter and return to oven for 10-12 minutes, until pastry is crisp and golden brown.

Arrange on a warmed serving dish garnished with sprigs of rosemary and orange slices.

*Serves 4.*

# SPICED GAMMON

| |
|---|
| 625 g (1¼ lb) gammon |
| 90 g (3 oz) creamed coconut |
| 6 teaspoons mango chutney |
| juice of 1 lime |
| 9 teaspoons sour cream |
| lime slices and parsley sprigs, to garnish |
| MARINADE: |
| 2 teaspoons cumin seeds, toasted |
| 1 teaspoon allspice berries |
| ½ teaspoon mustard seeds |
| ½ teaspoon white peppercorns |
| ½ teaspoon black peppercorns |
| 2 teaspoons grated lime peel |
| 30 g (1 oz/6 teaspoons) butter, melted |

Soak gammon in cold water for several hours or overnight. Drain and rinse in fresh water, then place in large saucepan, cover with water and bring to the boil.

Cover and simmer for 30 minutes. Remove gammon from saucepan and cool, then cut into thin strips.

To make marinade, mix cumin seeds, allspice, mustard seeds and peppercorns together in a pestle and mortar. Crush finely, then add lime peel and butter, working until the butter paste is well blended and smooth.

Rub marinade into gammon strips and place in a bowl. Cover with plastic wrap and leave in cool place for 2-3 hours.

Heat a non-stick frying pan, add meat and fry quickly for 2-3 minutes. Stir in coconut, chutney and lime juice, bring to the boil and cook for 2-3 minutes.

Remove pan from heat and stir in sour cream. Pour gammon mixture into a warmed serving dish and serve garnished with lime slices and parsley sprigs.

*Serves 4.*

## SPICED SKEWERED LAMB

| |
|---|
| **2 lamb neck fillets, about 500 g (1 lb), trimmed and cut into 7.5 cm (3 in) long strips** |
| MARINADE: |
| **1 teaspoon ground allspice** |
| **1 teaspoon grated fresh root ginger** |
| **3 teaspoons clear honey** |
| **6 teaspoons sherry vinegar** |
| **90 ml (3 fl oz/⅓ cup) apple juice** |
| **6 teaspoons chopped fresh mint** |
| **4 teaspoons olive oil** |
| GARNISH: |
| **fresh mint leaves** |
| **8 apple wedges** |
| **3 teaspoons lemon juice** |
| **8 lemon wedges** |

To make marinade, mix allspice, ginger, honey, sherry vinegar, apple juice, mint and oil together, stirring until evenly blended.

Add lamb strips and turn in marinade to coat each piece evenly. Cover with plastic wrap and leave in a cool place for 2-3 hours. Meanwhile, soak 8 fine wooden barbecue skewers in cold water. Prepare barbecue or preheat grill.

Thread several pieces of lamb onto each skewer and barbecue or grill for 2-3 minutes, turning once and brushing with more marinade if necessary.

Arrange lamb on a warmed serving plate, garnished with fresh mint leaves, wedges of apple tossed in lemon juice and lemon wedges.

Put remaining marinade in a saucepan, bring to the boil and pour into a dish. Serve with the lamb.

*Serves 4.*

# SWEET & SOUR SPARE RIBS

| |
|---|
| **12 pork spare ribs, about 750 g (1½ lb), trimmed** |
| **fresh herbs, to garnish** |
| MARINADE: |
| **3 teaspoons soy sauce** |
| **2 teaspoons clear honey** |
| **3 teaspoons dry sherry** |
| **9 teaspoons tomato purée (paste)** |
| **1 clove garlic, crushed** |
| **1 small chilli, seeded and chopped** |
| **2 teaspoons grated fresh root ginger** |
| **2.5 cm (1 in) cinnamon stick** |
| **6 cloves** |
| **½ teaspoon yellow mustard seeds** |
| **½ teaspoon salt** |
| **1 teaspoon black peppercorns** |

To make marinade, mix soy sauce, honey, sherry, tomato purée (paste), garlic, chilli and ginger together. In a pestle and mortar, crush the cinnamon, cloves, mustard seeds, salt and peppercorns until ground and blended. Stir the ground spice mixture into the marinade until evenly blended.

Pour marinade over spare ribs and turn to coat evenly. Cover with plastic wrap and leave in a cool place for 2-3 hours.

Meanwhile, prepare barbecue or preheat grill. Cook spare ribs for 5-8 minutes, until crisp, turning once and brushing with more marinade if necessary. Serve garnished with fresh herbs.

*Serves 4.*

# CHICKEN BITES

| | |
|---|---|
| 4 chicken breasts (fillets), about 750 g (1½ lb), cut into thin strips | |
| 24 kumquats | |
| winter savory, oregano sprigs and sliced kumquats, to garnish | |
| MARINADE: | |
| 155 g (5 oz/⅔ cup) strained Greek yogurt | |
| 2 teaspoons tomato purée (paste) | |
| 2 teaspoons Worcestershire sauce | |
| 6 teaspoons mango chutney | |
| ½ teaspoon salt | |
| ½ teaspoon black pepper | |
| 4 teaspoons chopped fresh oregano | |
| 4 teaspoons chopped fresh winter savory | |

Soak 12 wooden skewers in water.

To make marinade, mix yogurt, tomato purée (paste), Worcestershire sauce, chutney, salt, pepper and chopped oregano and winter savory together until well blended. Add chicken, stir to coat evenly and leave in cool place for 3 hours.

Meanwhile, prepare barbecue or preheat grill. Thread alternate slices of kumquat and pieces of chicken onto each kebab skewer.

Cook chicken bites for 5-8 minutes, turning once and brushing with marinade if necessary.

Serve hot, garnished with sprigs of winter savory, oregano and sliced kumquats.

*Serves 4.*

# CRISPY GRAPEFRUIT CHICKEN

**8 chicken thighs, about 1.25 kg (2 lb)**
**grapefruit segments and rosemary sprigs, to garnish**
MARINADE:
**3 teaspoons chopped fresh rosemary**
**3 teaspoons clear honey**
**60 ml (2 fl oz/¼ cup) olive oil**
**¾ teaspoon cayenne pepper**
**2 teaspoons finely grated grapefruit peel**
**6 teaspoons freshly squeezed grapefruit juice**

To make marinade, mix rosemary, honey, olive oil, cayenne, grapefruit peel and juice together until well blended.

Place chicken thighs in a shallow ovenproof dish, pour over marinade and turn chicken until evenly coated. Cover with plastic wrap and leave to marinate in a cool place for 3-4 hours.

Preheat oven to 220C (425F/Gas 7), or prepare a barbecue. Cook chicken for 20-25 minutes, until golden brown and skin is crisp, basting with marinade if necessary.

Arrange chicken on a serving plate and garnish with grapefruit segments and rosemary sprigs.

*Serves 4.*

# CURRIED DRUMSTICKS

| | |
|---|---|
| **8 chicken drumsticks** | |
| MARINADE: | |
| **1 teaspoon mild curry paste** | |
| **2 teaspoons finely grated lime peel** | |
| **3 teaspoons freshly squeezed lime juice** | |
| **30 g (1 oz/4 teaspoons) creamed coconut** | |
| **1 teaspoon clear honey** | |
| **½ teaspoon salt** | |
| **½ teaspoon black pepper** | |
| COATING: | |
| **60 g (2 oz/¼ cup) butter, softened** | |
| **1 clove garlic, crushed** | |
| **3 teaspoons chopped fresh coriander** | |
| **45 g (1½ oz/⅓ cup) fresh white breadcrumbs** | |

Wipe chicken drumsticks with absorbent kitchen paper.

To make marinade, mix curry paste, lime peel and juice, coconut, honey, salt and pepper together, stirring to form a paste.

Spread marinade evenly over each drumstick to coat. Place on a plate, cover with foil and leave in a cool place for 2 hours.

Preheat oven to 200C (400F/Gas 6). Blend together butter, garlic and coriander until soft and smooth. Place in an ovenproof dish and melt in oven.

Coat each drumstick evenly with breadcrumbs, then roll in butter mixture. Return to oven and cook for 30 minutes, until golden brown and juices run clear when drumsticks are pierced with tip of knife. Serve with a mixed salad.

*Makes 8.*

# DEVILLED TURKEY WINGS

4 turkey wings
90 g (3 oz/⅓ cup) butter, melted
watercress sprigs and tomato wedges, to garnish

MARINADE:
2 teaspoons ground ginger
2 teaspoons white pepper
2 teaspoons dry mustard
1 teaspoon salt
1 teaspoon curry powder
3 teaspoons soft brown sugar

SAUCE:
60 ml (2 fl oz/¼ cup) tomato sauce
6 teaspoons Worcestershire sauce
3 teaspoons soy sauce
6 teaspoons mango chutney

To make marinade, mix ginger, pepper, mustard, salt, curry powder and sugar together in a polythene bag. Shake until well mixed.

Place 1 turkey wing in the bag at a time and shake well to coat evenly with marinade. Place on a plate, cover with plastic wrap and leave in a cool place for 1 hour.

Preheat grill to moderate. Brush each turkey wing generously with butter, then grill for 10-12 minutes, turning frequently, until golden brown and turkey is cooked through. Arrange on a serving plate and keep warm.

To make the sauce, add tomato, Worcestershire and soy sauces to grill pan with chutney. Stir well, cooking under grill until sauce bubbles. Pour over turkey wings and garnish with watercress sprigs and tomato wedges.

*Serves 4.*

# CRANBERRY & ORANGE DUCK

| |
|---|
| 1 duck, about 2 kg (4 lb), cut into 4 joints |
| 2 teaspoons arrowroot |
| 2 teaspoons orange juice |
| MARINADE: |
| 125 g (4 oz/1 cup) cranberries |
| 8 teaspoons clear honey |
| 2 teaspoons finely grated orange peel |
| 6 teaspoons freshly squeezed orange juice |
| 155 ml (5 fl oz/⅔ cup) rosé wine |
| 4 teaspoons chopped fresh sage |
| ½ teaspoon each salt and black pepper |
| GARNISH: |
| orange slices |
| 4 teaspoons cranberries |
| fresh sage leaves |

Trim off excess fat and skin from duck joints to neaten.

To make marinade, place cranberries and honey in a small saucepan with 155 ml (5 fl oz/⅔ cup) water and boil. Cover and cook for 3 or 4 minutes, until tender. Press through a sieve to purée. Stir in remaining marinade ingredients.

Add duck joints to marinade and turn to coat evenly. Cover with plastic wrap and leave in a cool place for 4 hours or overnight.

Preheat oven to 220C (425F/Gas 7). Remove duck joints from marinade and arrange in an ovenproof dish. Cook for 45 minutes. Reduce temperature to 190C (375F/Gas 5). Pour marinade over duck, cover and cook for 40 minutes, or until duck is cooked and juices run clear when pierced with tip of knife. Place on a serving plate and keep warm.

Blend arrowroot and orange juice in a small pan. Pour off most of fat from marinade, add marinade to arrowroot mixture. Bring to boil, stirring, then cook gently 1 minute, until thick and clear. Pour sauce over duck, then garnish.

*Serves 4.*

# GOLDEN TURKEY

4 turkey steaks, about 500 g (1 lb)
fresh coriander leaves and lime wedges, to garnish

MARINADE:
12 cardamom pods
2 teaspoons coriander seeds
½ teaspoon yellow mustard seeds
1 clove garlic, crushed
3 teaspoons grated lime peel
½ teaspoon salt
½ teaspoon black pepper

COATING:
1 clove garlic, crushed
60 g (2 oz/¼ cup) butter
45 g (1½ oz/⅓ cup) plain potato crisps, crushed

To make marinade, remove seeds from cardamom pods and place in a pestle and mortar with coriander and mustard seeds. Crush until finely blended. Add garlic, lime peel, salt and pepper; mix well.

Cut a small slit in each turkey steak to make a pocket.

Spread marinade mixture over turkey steaks, rubbing well into the flesh. Place in dish, cover with plastic wrap and leave in a cool place for 2-3 hours.

Preheat oven to 220C (425F/Gas 7). Blend together remaining garlic and butter, beating well until smooth and soft. Spread each turkey steak evenly with half garlic butter, and fill each cavity with remainder.

Coat turkey steaks evenly in crushed crisps and arrange in a small roasting tin, cavity side uppermost. Cook for 15 minutes, until golden brown and crisp and cooked through.

Arrange on a serving plate and garnish with fresh coriander leaves and lime wedges.

*Serves 4.*

## TURKEY STROGANOFF

| |
|---|
| 3 turkey breast (fillets), about 750g (1½ lb), cut into thin slices |
| 30 g (1 oz/6 teaspoons) butter |
| 3 teaspoons olive oil |
| 185 g (6 oz) button mushrooms |
| 3 teaspoons lemon juice |
| 155 ml (5 fl oz/⅔ cup) pineapple juice |
| 155 ml (5 fl-oz/⅔ cup) chicken stock |
| 155 ml (5 fl oz/⅔ cup) single (light) cream |
| 1 egg yolk |
| flesh from ½ pineapple, chopped |
| 30 g (1 oz/½ cup) flaked almonds, toasted, and parsley sprigs, to garnish |
| MARINADE: |
| 6 teaspoons plain flour |
| ½ teaspoon ground cloves |
| 1 teaspoon grated nutmeg |
| ½ teaspoon salt |
| ½ teaspoon black pepper |
| 2 teaspoons grated lemon peel |

To make marinade, mix flour, cloves, nutmeg, salt, pepper and lemon peel together in a dish.

Add turkey pieces and turn in mixture to coat evenly. Cover with plastic wrap and a leave in a cool place for 1 hour.

Melt butter and oil in a frying pan. Add turkey and mushrooms and cook quickly, stirring occasionally. Stir in lemon and pineapple juices and stock and bring to the boil, then cover the pan and cook for 5 minutes.

Beat together cream and egg yolk, then stir cream into turkey and mushroom mixture and immediately remove from the heat.

Stir in half pineapple and pour mixture into a warmed serving dish. Garnish with the remaining chopped pineapple, flaked almonds and sprigs of parsley.

*Serves 4.*

# PHEASANT IN MADEIRA

| |
|---|
| 1 oven-ready pheasant |
| 30 g (1 oz/6 teaspoons) butter |
| 4 teaspoons plain flour |
| 6 teaspoons single (light) cream |
| MARINADE: |
| 1 teaspoon clear honey |
| 2 teaspoons finely grated grapefruit peel |
| 6 teaspoons chopped fresh purple basil |
| 6 teaspoons snipped fresh chives |
| 1 teaspoon dry mustard |
| ½ teaspoon salt |
| ½ teaspoon black pepper |
| 155 ml (5 fl oz/⅔ cup) Madeira |
| 6 teaspoons olive oil |
| 4 figs, cut into quarters |
| 125 g (4 oz/1 cup) cherries, stoned |
| GARNISH: |
| 1 fresh fig, sliced |
| 8 cherries |
| grapefruit segments |
| watercress sprigs |

Cut pheasant into 4 joints, trim off excess skin; remove wing bones.

To make marinade, mix honey, grapefruit peel, basil, chives, mustard, salt, pepper, Madeira and oil together, then add fruit.

Add joints to marinade turning to coat. Cover with plastic wrap and leave in a cool place for 4 hours.

Preheat oven to 180C (350F/Gas 4). Melt butter in a frying pan, take joints out of marinade and fry quickly to brown. Add marinade, bring to the boil and pour into casserole dish. Cook for 1 hour or until pheasant is tender and juices run clear when pricked with knife.

Arrange pheasant joints on a warmed serving dish and keep warm. Skim fat off marinade. Blend flour and cream, add to marinade and bring to boil, stirring, until thick. Cook gently for 2 minutes, pour over pheasant, then garnish.

*Serves 4.*

# POUSSIN PROVENÇAL

- 2 poussin, halved
- 1 red pepper (capsicum)
- 4 tomatoes, skinned, seeded and sliced
- fresh basil leaves, to garnish

MARINADE:

- 10 stoned olives, halved
- 5 anchovy fillets, well drained and chopped
- 9 teaspoons olive oil
- 9 teaspoons sweet sherry
- 1 clove garlic, crushed
- ½ teaspoon black pepper
- 6 teaspoons chopped fresh basil

To make marinade, mix olives, anchovies, oil, sherry, garlic, pepper and basil together, stirring until well mixed. Add poussin and turn in marinade to coat evenly. Cover with plastic wrap and leave in a cool place for 4 hours.

Preheat oven to 220C (425F/Gas 7). Place pepper (capsicum) on a baking sheet, place in oven and cook until skin is burnt and flesh is tender. Remove from oven and set aside to cool.

Lift poussin joints out of marinade and arrange in an ovenproof dish, spooning a little marinade over each.

Cook for 30-40 minutes, until golden brown, crisp and juices run clear when pricked with the tip of a knife. Keep warm.

Skin pepper (capsicum), cut into strips and place in a saucepan with tomatoes and remaining marinade. Bring to the boil, then cook gently for 5 minutes, stirring occasionally.

Pour the mixture into a warmed serving dish, arrange the poussin joints on top and garnish the dish with basil leaves.

*Serves* 4.

# STUFFED QUAIL IN PORT

4 oven-ready quails
fresh herb sprigs, to garnish

MARINADE:

90 ml (3 fl oz/⅓ cup) ruby port
6 teaspoons olive oil
3 teaspoons chopped fresh thyme
3 teaspoons chopped fresh oregano
3 teaspoons chopped fresh winter savory
1 clove garlic, crushed
½ teaspoon each salt and pepper

STUFFING:

30 g (1 oz) shallots
185 g (6 oz) button mushrooms
3 teaspoons chopped fresh parsley
125 g (4 oz) smoked streaky bacon, rinded and chopped

Cut feet and wing tips off each quail. Using kitchen scissors, split quails lengthwise, cutting through one side of backbone from neck to tail. Lay quails flat on a board with breast side uppermost and press to flatten, breaking backbone.

Make a slit between legs through flap of skin, then insert legs and pull through to secure. Loosen skin at breast end of bird for stuffing.

Mix marinade ingredients together, add quails and turn to coat. Cover and leave in a cool place 4 hours. To make stuffing, finely chop shallots, mushrooms and parsley. Add ½ teaspoon salt and pepper.

Heat a frying pan, and fry bacon until fat runs. Add mushroom mixture and fry until dry. Cool. Meanwhile, preheat grill.

Remove quail from marinade and insert stuffing under skin. Arrange on grill rack; brush with marinade. Cook for 10 minutes, turning once and basting with more marinade if necessary.

Arrange on a warmed serving dish and garnish with herbs.

*Serves 4.*

## BARBECUED TROUT IN LEAVES

| |
|---|
| 4 trout or 8 small red mullet, cleaned |
| 8 vine leaves |
| 1 teaspoon arrowroot |
| fennel sprigs and bay leaves, to garnish |
| MARINADE: |
| 6 teaspoons olive oil |
| shredded peel from 1 Seville orange |
| 6 teaspoons freshly squeezed orange juice |
| 1 clove garlic, crushed |
| 6 cardamom pod seeds, removed and crushed |
| ½ teaspoon salt |
| ½ teaspoon black pepper |
| 1 teaspoon Dijon mustard |
| 2 bay leaves |
| 3 teaspoons chopped fresh fennel |

Remove scales from the fish and cut off fins and gills using sharp scissors. Rinse under running water and dry on absorbent kitchen paper, then score the flesh on each side.

To make marinade, mix olive oil, orange peel, juice, garlic, cardamom seeds, salt, pepper, mustard, bay leaves and fennel together.

Immerse fish in marinade and turn to coat evenly. Cover with plastic wrap and leave in a cool place for 1 hour.

Preheat a hot grill. Take fish out of marinade and loosely wrap each in a vine leaf. Arrange fish on grill rack and cook for 6 minutes, turning once.

Unwrap each fish and arrange on a serving plate. Add juices from pan to remaining marinade and blend together with arrowroot. Put in a saucepan and bring to the boil, stirring, and cook for 1 minute, until thickened and glossy.

Pour sauce over fish and garnish with fennel and bay leaves.

*Serves 4.*

# BARBECUED SARDINES

| |
|---|
| 8 small sardines |
| MARINADE: |
| 90 g (3 oz/⅓ cup) strained Greek yogurt |
| ½ teaspoon Tabasco sauce |
| ½ teaspoon cayenne pepper |
| 3 teaspoons tomato purée (paste) |
| 60 ml (2 fl oz/¼ cup) sherry |
| ½ teaspoon salt |
| ¼ teaspoon black pepper |
| 1 teaspoon caster sugar |
| 4 teaspoons chopped fresh basil |
| 2 teaspoons snipped fresh chives |
| 2 teaspoons finely grated lemon peel |
| GARNISH: |
| herb sprigs |
| chive flowers, if desired |
| lemon wedges |

Wash and clean sardines very gently as these fish need careful handling; remove heads if desired. Dry well on kitchen paper.

To make marinade, mix yogurt, Tabasco sauce, cayenne, tomato purée (paste), sherry, salt, pepper, sugar, basil, chives and lemon peel together, stirring until evenly blended. Pour into a large shallow dish.

Add sardines 1 at a time and turn gently in marinade to coat evenly. Cover with plastic wrap and leave in a cool place for 1-2 hours.

Meanwhile, prepare barbecue or preheat grill. Arrange sardines on a fish or grill rack and cook for 5-6 minutes, turning only once, until crisp, brushing with more marinade if necessary.

Serve on a hot platter, garnished with fresh sprigs of herbs, chive flowers, if desired, and thin lemon wedges.

*Serves 4.*

**Variation:** If sardines are unavailable, use small trout or sprats.

# BUTTERED HERB SOLE FILLETS

- 8 Dover sole fillets, cut in half lengthwise
- 125 g (4 oz/½ cup) unsalted butter, softened
- 4 teaspoons chopped fresh tarragon
- 4 teaspoons plain flour
- 6 teaspoons single (light) cream
- fennel sprigs, to garnish

MARINADE:

- 250 ml (8 fl oz/1 cup) dry white wine
- 3 teaspoons chopped fresh fennel
- 1 eating apple, peeled and grated
- 2 teaspoons caster sugar
- ½ teaspoon salt
- ½ teaspoon cayenne pepper

To make marinade, mix wine, fennel, apple, sugar, salt and cayenne together in a casserole or shallow flameproof dish, stirring until well blended.

Add sole fillets and turn in marinade to coat evenly. Cover with plastic wrap and leave the fish in a cool place for 2 hours.

In a bowl, blend together butter and tarragon. Lift sole fillets out of marinade and lay flat on a board. Spread half of each fillet with herbed butter, then roll up firmly and secure each with cocktail stick.

Arrange rolled fillets in dish with marinade, cover and cook over a gentle heat for 5-6 minutes, until fish is cooked through and flakes easily. Lift fillets out carefully, arrange on a warm serving dish and keep warm.

Blend flour and cream together in a bowl, then strain marinade into bowl, stirring well. Return to saucepan, bring to the boil and cook for 1 minute. Pour sauce around fish fillets and garnish with fennel sprigs.

*Serves* 4-5.

## FRENCH COUNTRY COD STEAKS

| |
|---|
| 4 middle-cut cod steaks, 2.5 cm (1 in) thick |
| 30 g (1 oz/6 teaspoons) butter |
| 15 g (½ oz/6 teaspoons) plain flour |
| tarragon sprigs, to garnish |
| MARINADE: |
| 1 red pepper (capsicum) |
| 1 yellow pepper (capsicum) |
| 16 black olives, stoned |
| 4 tomatoes, skinned, seeded and sliced |
| 2 courgettes (zucchini), sliced |
| 1 red onion, sliced |
| 1 clove garlic, crushed |
| 6 teaspoons olive oil |
| 155 ml (5 fl oz/⅔ cup) strong cider |
| ½ teaspoon salt |
| ½ teaspoon black pepper |
| 1 teaspoon French mustard |
| 4 teaspoons chopped fresh tarragon |

To make marinade, place peppers (capsicums) on a grill rack and cook for 10 minutes, turning occasionally, until skins have charred and flesh is tender. Cool, then peel off skins, and remove stalks and seeds. Cut peppers (capsicums) into strips and place in an ovenproof dish.

Add olives, tomatoes, courgettes (zucchini), onion, garlic, oil, cider, salt, pepper, mustard and tarragon, stirring until well mixed.

Immerse cod steaks in marinade and turn to coat evenly. Cover and leave in a cool place for 1 hour.

Preheat oven to 200C (400F/Gas 6). Cook cod steaks in marinade for 25-30 minutes, until cooked and flake easily. Lift out on to a plate and remove bones and skin.

Blend butter and flour together, stir into marinade, then bring to the boil and cook for 2 minutes.

Arrange cod steaks on a serving plate, pour over marinade and garnish with sprigs of tarragon.

*Serves 4.*

# HONEY GINGER PRAWNS

8 king prawns or scampi, heads and shells removed
vegetable oil for deep frying
1 teaspoon arrowroot
satsuma wedges and herb sprigs, to garnish
MARINADE:
3 teaspoons light soy sauce
3 teaspoons dry sherry
2 teaspoons finely grated satsuma peel
3 teaspoons satsuma juice
1 clove garlic, crushed
2 teaspoons clear honey
½ teaspoon black pepper
BATTER:
125 g (4 oz/¼ cup) plain flour
¼ teaspoon salt
¼ teaspoon dry mustard
¼ teaspoon ground black pepper
4 teaspoons olive oil
100 ml (3½ fl oz/⅓ cup) lager
2 egg whites

Mix marinade ingredients together, add prawns or scampi and turn to coat. Cover with plastic wrap and leave in cool place for 2 hours.

To make batter, place flour, salt, mustard and pepper in a bowl and make a well in centre. Add oil and the lager and beat to form a smooth batter. Cover with plastic wrap and leave in cool place for 30 minutes.

Remove prawns or scampi from marinade and drain well. Stiffly whisk egg whites and fold into batter. Half-fill a deep-fat frying pan with oil and heat to 180C (350F). Hold prawns or scampi by tails and dip into batter, then fry for 2-3 minutes, until golden brown. Drain on kitchen paper and keep warm.

Blend arrowroot with marinade in a small pan and bring to boil, stirring, then cook for 30 seconds. Arrange 2 prawns on each plate and pour on a little sauce. Garnish.

*Serves 4.*

# SPICY SCALLOPS

- 12 scallops, cleaned
- 90 ml (3 fl oz/⅓ cup) cider
- 15 g (½ oz/6 teaspoons) plain flour
- 15 g (½ oz/3 teaspoons) butter
- 2 teaspoons finely grated lemon peel
- 6 teaspoons lemon juice
- 3 teaspoons chopped fresh dill

MARINADE:

- 90 ml (3 fl oz/⅓ cup) sour cream
- ½ teaspoon ground cumin
- ½ teaspoon ground cinnamon
- ½ teaspoon turmeric
- 1 teaspoon grated fresh root ginger
- 2 teaspoons clear honey
- ½ teaspoon salt
- ½ teaspoon black pepper

GARNISH:

- toast triangles
- dill sprigs
- lemon wedges

Place scallops and cider in a saucepan; poach gently for 1 minute.

To make marinade, mix sour cream, cumin, cinnamon, turmeric, ginger, honey, salt and pepper together, stirring until well blended.

Lift scallops out of liquor with a slotted spoon and slice thinly. Add to marinade and turn to coat evenly. Cover with plastic wrap and leave for 1 hour.

Whisk flour and butter into poaching liquor in saucepan, then bring to the boil, whisking, until sauce thickens. Stir in scallops, marinade, lemon peel and juice and dill and cook gently until mixture comes to boil, stirring occasionally.

Divide scallops between 6 shells or individual serving dishes and garnish with triangles of toast, dill sprigs and lemon wedges.

*Serves 6.*

# SEAFOOD KEBABS

375 g (12 oz) thick end monkfish, cut into bite-size pieces
3 plaice fillets, cut into thin strips
3 courgettes (zucchini), cut into bite-size pieces
1 small yellow pepper (capsicum), seeded and cut into bite-size pieces
12 large prawns, peeled

MARINADE:
¼ teaspoon powdered saffron
finely grated peel of 1 lime
3 teaspoons freshly squeezed lime juice
3 teaspoons clear honey
1 teaspoon green peppercorns, crushed
6 teaspoons white vermouth
90 ml (3 fl oz/⅓ cup) grapeseed oil
½ teaspoon salt
½ teaspoon black pepper
6 fresh bay leaves
3 teaspoons chopped fresh dill

GARNISH:
bay leaves
6 lime wedges
dill sprigs

To make marinade, mix all the ingredients together. Add monkfish, plaice, courgettes (zucchini), pepper (capsicum) and prawns to marinade. Turn vegetables and fish carefully in marinade to coat evenly. Cover with plastic wrap and leave in a cool place for 1 hour. Meanwhile, soak 6 fine wooden skewers in cold water. Prepare barbecue or preheat grill.

Thread alternate pieces of each fish, with courgette (zucchini) and pepper (capsicum) in between, on to skewers with a bay leaf at the end of each. Cook for 5-8 minutes, turning only once and brushing with more marinade if necessary.

Arrange on a warmed serving dish and serve at once, garnished with fresh bay leaves, lime wedges and sprigs of dill.

*Serves* 6.

# SALMON IN FILO PASTRY

| |
|---|
| 4 salmon steaks, about 500 g (1 lb), skinned and boned |
| 90 g (3 oz/⅓ cup) unsalted butter |
| 185 g (6 oz) oyster mushrooms, thinly sliced |
| 4 sheets filo pastry, thawed if frozen |
| 2 teaspoons arrowroot |
| 3 teaspoons single (light) cream |
| fennel sprigs and pink peppercorns, to garnish |
| MARINADE: |
| 2 teaspoons light soft brown sugar |
| 6 teaspoons rosé wine |
| 6 teaspoons raspberry vinegar |
| 2 teaspoons pink peppercorns, crushed |
| 4 teaspoons chopped fresh fennel |
| 4 teaspoons chopped fresh oregano |

Mix the marinade ingredients together, pour over the salmon in a shallow dish and turn to coat evenly. Cover with plastic wrap and leave in a cool place for 1 hour.

Preheat oven to 200C (400F/Gas 6). Melt 30 g (1 oz/6 teaspoons) butter in a small saucepan, add mushrooms, reserving a few for garnish, and fry quickly. Drain, reserving the liquid, then cool.

Melt remaining butter. Brush each sheet of filo pastry with melted butter and fold in half. Take 1 salmon steak at a time, drain well and place in centre of 1 folded piece of pastry. Top with one quarter mushroom slices and wrap up neatly. Place on a buttered baking sheet; repeat to make 4 parcels. Brush with remaining butter.

Cook for 15 minutes, until pastry is crisp and lightly browned. Mix marinade, mushroom liquid and arrowroot in a pan. Bring to boil and cook 1 minute; stir in cream.

Garnish salmon and serve with cream sauce.

*Serves 4.*

# MUSSELS WITH BASIL SAUCE

| | |
|---|---|
| **32 fresh mussels** |
| **parsley sprigs or basil, to garnish** |
| **MARINADE:** |
| **9 teaspoons olive oil** |
| **3 teaspoons raspberry vinegar** |
| **3 teaspoons chopped fresh parsley** |
| **2 teaspoons pink peppercorns, crushed** |
| **½ teaspoon salt** |
| **½ teaspoon black pepper** |
| **1 teaspoon Dijon mustard** |
| **SAUCE:** |
| **60 g (2 oz/¼ cup) butter, softened** |
| **15 g (½ oz/6 teaspoons) plain flour** |
| **6 teaspoons chopped fresh basil** |
| **6 teaspoons single (light) cream** |

Scrub mussels thoroughly under running water and scrape shells clean with a small knife if necessary. Pull beards or thin strands off from side of shells. Discard any that are open.

Place mussels in a stainless steel saucepan. Cover and heat very gently until all shells have opened. Remove pan from heat; discard any shells that have not opened.

To make marinade, mix oil, vinegar, parsley, peppercorns, salt, pepper and mustard together, stirring until well blended. Pour marinade over mussels, stir well and leave for 1 hour.

Return mussels to heat, bring to the boil and cook for 1 minute. Take mussels, 1 at a time, remove empty side of shell and arrange remainder in a shallow serving dish.

To make sauce, blend together butter and flour, then add basil and whisk into marinade in saucepan. Add 90 ml (3 fl oz/⅓ cup) water and bring to the boil.

Stir in cream, then pour sauce over mussels in dish. Garnish with fresh parsley sprigs or basil leaves.

*Serves* 4-6.

# TROUT IN ASPIC

| |
|---|
| 4 trout, each about 250 g (8 oz), rinsed |
| 90 ml (3 fl oz/⅓ cup) Mayonnaise, page 46 |
| 2 teaspoons tomato purée (paste) |
| 6 teaspoons lemon juice |
| 15 g (½ oz/3 teaspoons) gelatine |
| 1 cucumber, very thinly sliced |
| lemon wedges, to garnish |
| MARINADE: |
| 1 red onion, sliced |
| 60 g (2 oz/½ cup) bulb fennel, chopped |
| 2 bay leaves |
| 6 teaspoons chopped fresh parsley |
| 315 ml (10 fl oz/1¼ cups) dry white wine |
| ½ teaspoon each salt and black pepper |

Mix the marinade, then pour over trout in a shallow ovenproof dish. Cover and leave in a cool place for 2-3 hours. Mix mayonnaise and tomato purée (paste) together.

Preheat oven to 190C (375F/Gas 5). Cook trout for 15-20 minutes, until flesh flakes easily. Cool. Lift 1 trout out of marinade, peel off skin and remove fins, leaving head and tail intact. Remove top fillet; place lower fillet on a plate. Cut through centre bone of lower fillet at head and tail end, then lift off bones. Spread fillet with one quarter mayonnaise; replace top fillet. Repeat with remaining trout.

Strain marinade into a jug and make up to 440 ml (14 fl oz/1¾ cups) with water. Add lemon juice and blend 9 teaspoons of marinade with gelatine in a small bowl. Melt over pan of hot water, stir into remaining marinade; leave until beginning to thicken.

Sprinkle cucumber with salt, leave 15 minutes, rinse and pat dry. Brush trout with marinade and arrange overlapping cucumber slices to cover. Glaze with marinade; leave to set. Garnish.

*Serves 4.*

# ASPARAGUS & AVOCADO SALAD

| |
|---|
| 500 g (1 lb) asparagus spears |
| 1 ripe avocado |
| 4 teaspoons chopped pistachio nuts or walnuts |
| fennel sprigs and orange segments, to garnish |
| MARINADE: |
| 125 ml (4 fl oz/½ cup) walnut oil |
| 6 teaspoons freshly squeezed orange juice |
| 2 teaspoons grated orange peel |
| 2 teaspoons light soft brown sugar |
| ½ teaspoon salt |
| ½ teaspoon black pepper |
| 2 teaspoons Dijon mustard |
| 6 teaspoons chopped fresh fennel |

Trim asparagus spears and, using a sharp knife, peel outside skin off each stem. Cook asparagus in large shallow saucepan of boiling salted water for 5-8 minutes, until tender. Drain and cool.

To make marinade, mix oil, orange juice, peel, sugar, salt, pepper, mustard and fennel together, stirring until well blended.

Place asparagus spears in a shallow dish, pour over marinade and turn each spear in marinade to coat evenly. Cover with plastic wrap and leave in a cool place for 1 hour or until ready to serve.

Lift out asparagus and arrange on 4 individual serving plates. Peel and dice avocado and add to marinade with pistachios or walnuts, turning gently.

Spoon avocado and nut mixture over centres of asparagus spears and garnish with sprigs of fennel and orange segments.

*Serves 4.*

# AUBERGINE-FILLED MUSHROOMS

8 mushroom cups, each 5 cm (2 in) across
basil leaves or tomato wedges, to garnish

MARINADE:
3 tomatoes, skinned and seeded
60 ml (2 fl oz/¼ cup) olive oil
¼ teaspoon salt
¼ teaspoon black pepper
1 teaspoon sugar
freshly squeezed juice of 1 orange
4 teaspoons chopped fresh basil

FILLING:
1 aubergine (eggplant)
1 clove garlic, crushed
90 g (3 oz/⅓ cup) cream cheese

Remove stalks from mushrooms. Arrange mushrooms in a dish.

To make marinade, place mushroom stalks in a food processor fitted with a metal blade with tomatoes, oil, salt, pepper, sugar, orange juice and basil and process until smooth.

Spoon marinade into each mushroom cup and pour remainder into dish. Cover with plastic wrap and leave in a cool place for 1 hour.

Meanwhile, preheat oven to 220C (425F/Gas 7). Make the filling, bake aubergine (eggplant) for 15-20 minutes, until skin looks burnt and flesh is tender. Cool, then peel away skin and scrape flesh into food processor.

Add garlic, cream cheese, salt and pepper; process until smooth.

Remove plastic wrap and bake mushrooms for 5 minutes. Spoon aubergine (eggplant) mixture into each cup, then return to the oven for a further 5-8 minutes, until filling has set and the mushrooms are tender.

Serve as a snack or starter, garnished with basil leaves or tomato wedges.

*Serves 4.*

# CRISPY COATED VEGETABLES

| |
|---|
| 8 cup mushrooms, halved |
| 2 courgettes (zucchini), cut into 1 cm (½ in) slices |
| 125 g (4 oz) mange tout or dwarf French beans, topped and tailed |
| 1 fennel bulb, broken into bite-size pieces |
| 250 g (8 oz) cauliflower or broccoli, broken into flowerets |
| vegetable oil for deep frying |
| lime wedges and fennel sprigs, to garnish |
| MARINADE: |
| 8 teaspoons chopped fresh basil |
| 2 teaspoons finely grated lime peel |
| 3 teaspoons freshly squeezed lime juice |
| 1 teaspoon finely grated fresh root ginger |
| 1 teaspoon caster sugar |
| 6 teaspoons olive oil |
| ½ teaspoon each salt and black pepper |
| BATTER: |
| 125 g ( 4 oz/1 cup) self-raising flour |
| 1 egg, separated |

To make marinade, mix basil, lime peel and juice, ginger, sugar, oil, salt and pepper together, stirring well.

Add all vegetables to marinade and turn to coat evenly. Cover with plastic wrap and leave for 1 hour.

To make batter, place flour in a bowl and make a well in centre. Add egg yolk and gradually stir in 155 ml (5 fl oz/⅔) cup water, beating until smooth. Stiffly whisk egg white and fold into batter.

Half-fill a deep-fat frying pan with oil and heat to 180C (350F). Take 1 piece of vegetable at a time and dip into batter to coat evenly, then place in oil. Fry about 12 pieces of vegetable at a time until lightly browned and crisp. Drain well on absorbent kitchen paper. Repeat with rest of vegetables.

Arrange on a serving plate, garnish and serve with a spicy dip or dressing.

*Serves 4.*

# CURRIED VEGETABLES

| | |
|---|---|
| 315 g (10 oz) kohlrabi, cubed | |
| 250 g (8 oz) celery, sliced | |
| 125 g (4 oz) broccoli or cauliflower, broken into flowerets | |
| 185 g (6 oz) carrots, cubed | |
| 250 g (8 oz) potato or Jerusalem artichokes, cubed | |
| coriander and celery leaves, to garnish | |
| MARINADE: | |
| 2 teaspoons cumin seeds | |
| 2 teaspoons coriander seeds | |
| 6 cardamom pods | |
| 2 teaspoons turmeric | |
| 2 teaspoons garam masala | |
| ½ teaspoon each salt and black pepper | |
| 1 clove garlic | |
| SAUCE: | |
| 60 g (2 oz/½ cup) plain flour | |
| 60 g (2 oz/¼ cup) butter | |
| 155 ml (5 fl oz/⅔ cup) milk | |
| 315 ml (10 fl oz/1¼ cups) vegetable stock | |

To make marinade, place cumin and coriander seeds and seeds from cardamom pods into a pestle and mortar; crush finely. Add turmeric, garam masala, salt, pepper and garlic, working together in pestle and mortar until evenly blended.

Cook vegetables in boiling salted water for 2-3 minutes, until slightly tender. Drain.

Place vegetables in a bowl, add marinade mixture and toss until evenly coated. Leave for 2 hours.

To make sauce, mix flour, butter, milk and vegetable stock together in a saucepan. Bring to the boil, whisking until sauce thickens. Add vegetables, stir gently and bring back to the boil, then cover and simmer for 20 minutes or until vegetables are just tender.

Pour curried vegetables into a serving dish and garnish with coriander and celery leaves.

*Serves 4.*

# HERB CUCUMBER FRAIS

| |
|---|
| 1 cucumber |
| 250 g (8 oz/1 cup) fromage frais |
| dill sprigs and chive flowers, to garnish |
| MARINADE: |
| 4 teaspoons chopped fresh tarragon |
| 4 teaspoons chopped fresh dill |
| 4 teaspoons snipped fresh chives |
| ½ teaspoon salt |
| ½ teaspoon black pepper |
| ½ teaspoon dry mustard |
| 6 teaspoons red vermouth |

Using a canelle cutter, cut off thin strips of cucumber peel to make a ridge effect. Cut cucumber in half lengthwise, scoop out seeds and cut cucumber into 0.5 cm (¼ in) slices.

Bring 155 ml (5 fl oz/⅔ cup) water to boil in a pan, add cucumber and cook for 1 minute. Drain.

To make marinade, mix tarragon, dill, chives, salt, pepper, mustard and vermouth together. Add cucumber and turn gently in marinade to coat. Cover with plastic wrap and leave in a cool place for 2 hours.

Just before serving, gently stir in fromage frais until evenly mixed. Place cucumber mixture in a serving dish and garnish with sprigs of dill and chive flowers.

*Serves 4.*

# MARINATED PEPPERS

2 green peppers (capsicums)
2 yellow peppers (capsicums)
2 red peppers (capsicums)
MARINADE:
90 ml (3 fl oz/⅓ cup) almond oil
3 teaspoons cider vinegar
3 teaspoons clear honey
½ teaspoon salt
½ teaspoon black pepper
1 teaspoon Dijon mustard
1 teaspoon tomato purée (paste)
2 teaspoons snipped fresh chives
2 teaspoons chopped fresh parsley
2 teaspoons chopped fresh marjoram
2 teaspoons chopped fresh winter savory
1 clove garlic, crushed
1 teaspoon sugar

Preheat grill to hot or oven to 220C (425F/Gas 7). Place peppers (capsicums) under grill or on baking sheet and cook for 15-20 minutes, until the skins are black and charred on all sides and flesh is tender.

Plunge peppers (capsicums) into cold water to cool quickly, then drain and peel off skins, removing stalks and seeds. Cut each pepper (capsicum) into 1 cm (½ in) strips and arrange all the strips in a shallow serving dish.

To make marinade, mix oil, cider vinegar, honey, salt, pepper, mustard, tomato purée (paste), chives, parsley, marjoram, savory, garlic and sugar together, stirring until well blended.

Pour over peppers (capsicums) and turn to coat evenly. Cover with plastic wrap and leave in a cool place for 1-2 hours.

Serve as an accompaniment to grilled or barbecued meat or fish, or as a salad.

*Serves 4.*

# MARINATED STUFFED LEAVES

8 small spinach leaves
8 small Chinese leaves
8 small radicchio leaves
1 yellow pepper (capsicum)
marjaram and parsley sprigs, to garnish

MARINADE:
1 teaspoon finely grated orange peel
3 teaspoons freshly squeezed orange juice
90 ml (3 fl oz/⅓ cup) olive oil
3 teaspoons chopped fresh marjoram
½ teaspoon each salt and black pepper
1 teaspoon Dijon mustard
1 teaspoon caster sugar

FILLING:
250 g (8 oz/1 cup) full fat soft cheese
1 clove garlic, crushed
6 teaspoons chopped fresh parsley

Plunge spinach leaves into boiling water for 30 seconds; refresh in cold water. Drain well. Repeat with Chinese and radicchio leaves.

To make marinade, mix all the ingredients together. Pour one-third into a bowl and add radicchio leaves, turning to coat. Place spinach and Chinese leaves in remaining marinade. Cover and leave in a cool place for 2 hours.

To make filling, beat cheese, garlic and parsley together.

Preheat grill, and grill pepper (capsicum) until skin is charred and flesh is tender. Peel and remove stalk and seeds, then purée in a food processor or blender.

Drain leaves, reserving marinade. Take 1 leaf at a time and spread out flat on a board. Place 1 teaspoonful of cheese in centre, fold in edges and roll up firmly. Repeat until all the leaves are used. Place in a serving dish.

Mix pepper (capsicum) and remaining marinade together and pour around leaves in dish. Garnish.

*Serves 4.*

# MIXED VEGETABLE KEBABS

| | |
|---|---|
| 375 g (12 oz) aubergine (eggplant), cut into bite-size pieces | |
| 125 g (4 oz) red pepper (capsicum), seeded and cut into 2 cm (¾ in) cubes | |
| 125 g (4 oz) yellow pepper (capsicum), seeded and cut into 2 cm (¾ in) cubes | |
| 4 small courgettes (zucchini), trimmed and cut into 1 cm (½ in) slices | |
| 8 shallots, quartered | |
| 16 button mushrooms | |
| 16 cherry tomatoes | |
| oregano and parsley sprigs, to garnish | |
| MARINADE: | |
| 90 ml (3 fl oz/⅓ cup) olive oil | |
| 3 teaspoons raspberry vinegar | |
| ½ teaspoon each salt and black pepper | |
| 1 teaspoon dry mustard | |
| 3 teaspoons light soft brown sugar | |
| 3 teaspoons chopped fresh oregano | |
| 3 teaspoons chopped fresh parsley | |

To make marinade, mix oil, vinegar, salt, pepper, mustard, sugar, chopped oregano and parsley together, stirring until well blended.

Put aubergine (eggplant) in a colander or sieve over a bowl, sprinkle with salt, cover with a plate, weight the top and leave for 30 minutes. Rinse thoroughly to remove salt, then press out water.

Add all vegetables to marinade and turn vegetables carefully to coat completely. Cover with plastic wrap and leave to marinate in a cool place for 1 hour.

Meanwhile, soak 8 wooden barbecue skewers. Prepare barbecue or preheat grill.

Thread a mixture of vegetables on to the skewers. Cook 3-5 minutes, brushing with marinade until just tender.

Arrange on a serving dish, garnished with fresh oregano and parsley sprigs.

*Serves 4.*

# RATATOUILLE

- 1 aubergine (eggplant), thinly sliced
- salt
- 90 ml (3 fl oz/⅓ cup) olive oil
- 1 red pepper (capsicum), seeded and thinly sliced
- 1 yellow pepper (capsicum), seeded and thinly sliced
- 2 onions, thinly sliced
- 3 courgettes (zucchini), thinly sliced
- 3 tomatoes, skinned, seeded and thinly sliced
- coriander, basil or parsley, to garnish

MARINADE:

- 6 teaspoons dry red wine
- 1 clove garlic, crushed
- 6 teaspoons chopped fresh coriander
- 6 teaspoons chopped fresh basil
- 6 teaspoons chopped fresh parsley
- 1 teaspoon Dijon mustard
- ½ teaspoon salt
- ½ teaspoon black pepper

Arrange aubergine (eggplant) in a colander or sieve over a bowl. Sprinkle salt between layers, cover with a plate, weight down and leave 30 minutes. Rinse under cold running water and dry the slices on kitchen paper.

Heat oil in a large frying pan, add aubergine (eggplant), peppers (capsicums), onions and courgettes (zucchini) and fry gently 4-5 minutes, stirring occasionally, until almost tender. Add tomatoes and cook for 3-4 minutes, until all the vegetables are tender.

To make marinade, mix wine, garlic, coriander, basil, parsley, mustard, salt and pepper together. Add vegetables and turn in marinade until well coated. Set aside until cold.

Pour into a serving dish and garnish with fresh coriander, parsley or basil leaves.

*Serves* 6.

# SPICED OKRA

| | |
|---|---|
| 375 g (12 oz) okra, stalks removed | |
| 4 tomatoes, skinned, seeded and chopped | |
| 90 g (3 oz/⅓ cup) strained Greek yogurt | |
| coriander sprigs, to garnish | |
| MARINADE: | |
| 1 red chilli, seeded and chopped | |
| 1 onion, finely chopped | |
| 1 clove garlic, crushed | |
| 1 teaspoon ground cumin | |
| 1 teaspoon ground coriander | |
| ½ teaspoon salt | |
| ½ teaspoon black pepper | |
| 1 teaspoon sugar | |
| 6 teaspoons olive oil | |

To make marinade, mix chilli, onion, garlic, cumin, coriander, salt, pepper, sugar and oil together, stirring until thoroughly blended.

Add okra to marinade and turn gently until evenly coated. Cover with plastic wrap and leave in a cool place for 1 hour.

Put tomatoes and 155 ml (5 fl oz/ ⅔ cup) water in a saucepan and bring to the boil. Add okra and marinade and return to the boil, stirring carefully. Cover and cook for 15-20 minutes, until okra is tender.

Pour mixture into a shallow serving dish, add yogurt and stir gently to swirl yogurt. Serve hot or cold, garnished with coriander sprigs.

*Serves 4.*

# BRANDIED FRUIT CRÊPES

| |
|---|
| **185 g (6 oz/¾ cup) caster sugar** |
| **4 strips pared lemon peel** |
| **125 g (4 oz) kumquats** |
| **3 nectarines, sliced** |
| **butter for frying** |
| **60 ml (2 fl oz/¼ cup) apricot brandy** |
| **mint leaves or tiny flowers, to decorate** |
| BATTER: |
| **125 g (4 oz/1 cup) plain flour** |
| **155 ml (5 fl oz/⅔ cup) milk** |
| **1 egg** |

Gently heat sugar, lemon peel and 315 ml (10 fl oz/1¼ cups) water in a saucepan until sugar has dissolved. Add kumquats and bring to the boil, then cover and cook gently for 5 minutes, until tender.

Pour kumquats into a bowl, add nectarines and set aside until cold.

Meanwhile, to make batter, place flour in a bowl and mix milk and egg together with 155 ml (5 fl oz/⅔ cup) water in a jug, whisking until well blended. Make a well in centre of flour and add half milk mixture, beating well with a wooden spoon. Add remaining milk, beating well.

Melt enough butter to lightly grease a small frying pan. Pour in enough batter to just thinly coat base of pan and swirl pan to spread the batter. Cook for about 1 minute on each side.

Place crêpe on a plate covered with kitchen paper; repeat to make 10-12 crêpes. Cover and keep warm.

Strain syrup from fruit into a saucepan, boil rapidly for 3-4 minutes, until thick. Cool slightly, stir in brandy and pour over fruit.

Fold crêpes into 4 making a triangle and serve with kumquats, nectarines and syrup. Decorate with mint leaves or tiny flowers.

*Serves 4.*

# FIG & PORT ICE CREAM

| |
|---|
| **125 g (4 oz/½ cup) caster sugar** |
| **155 ml (5 fl oz/⅔ cup) ruby port** |
| **4 cm (1½ in) cinnamon stick** |
| **6 fresh figs** |
| **4 teaspoons freshly squeezed lime juice** |
| **315 ml (10 fl oz/1¼ cups) double (thick) cream** |
| **fresh fig slices and mint leaves, to decorate** |

Place sugar and port in a saucepan and heat gently, stirring occasionally, until sugar has melted. Bring to the boil, then add cinnamon stick and figs, cover and cook very gently for 5 minutes. Leave the figs in the marinade, still covered, until they are completely cold.

Transfer figs and liquor to a food processor fitted with a metal blade and process until smooth.

Pour mixture into a sieve over a bowl and rub through using a wooden spoon. Stir in lime juice.

Whip cream until thick, then fold into fig purée until evenly blended. Pour mixture into a plastic container, cover and freeze for 1-2 hours, until almost frozen.

Return mixture to food processor and process until thick and smooth. Return to plastic container and freeze until firm. Scoop ice cream to serve, then decorate.

*Serves 4.*

# GINGERED MELON CUP

- **2 grapefruit, halved and segmented with half shells reserved**
- **1 ogen or charentais melon, halved and flesh cut into small balls and half shells reserved**
- **125 g (4 oz) strawberries, sliced**
- **125 g (4 oz) black grapes, seeded**
- **ginger mint sprigs, to decorate**

MARINADE:

- **155 ml (5 fl oz/⅔ cup) ginger wine**
- **60 g (2 oz/¼ cup) caster sugar**
- **8 teaspoons chopped fresh ginger mint**
- **4 teaspoons chopped preserved ginger in heavy syrup**

To make marinade, mix ginger wine, sugar, mint and preserved ginger together, stirring until blended.

Put the fruit in a bowl and pour over the marinade. Turn fruit carefully in marinade. Cover with plastic wrap and chill until required.

Meanwhile, cut edge of each grapefruit and melon shell into a zig-zag pattern using small sharp scissors. Fill each shell with fruit and marinade mixture. Decorate tops with sprigs of ginger mint.

*Serves 6.*

**Note:** Use a Parisienne cutter, available from kitchen shops, to make the melon balls, or a teaspoon.

# JEWELLED FRUIT JELLY

470 ml (15 fl oz/2 cups) red grape juice
470 ml (15 fl oz/2 cups) white grape juice
6 teaspoons gelatine
1 star fruit, sliced
125 g (4 oz) white seedless grapes
125 g (4 oz) cherries, stoned
125 g (4 oz) strawberries, halved and sliced
strawberry leaves and flowers, to decorate

MARINADE:
4 teaspoons orange flower water or Cointreau
4 teaspoons rosewater or kirsch
8 teaspoons icing sugar

Pour red and white grape juices into separate bowls. Sprinkle gelatine over 90 ml (3 fl oz/⅓ cup) water in a bowl and stir. Dissolve over a pan of hot water until clear, then stir half into each bowl of juice.

To make marinade, pour flower water or Cointreau, and rosewater or kirsch onto separate plates; sift half the icing sugar on to each. Add star fruit and grapes to flower water or Cointreau, and cherries and strawberries to rosewater or kirsch. Cover and leave 30 minutes.

Using a 1.5 litre (2½ pint/6 cup) fluted mould or 8 individual moulds, pour 1 cm (½ in) white juice into mould. Cool until just setting.

Arrange one-third star fruit and grapes over jelly, spoon over white juice to cover; leave until set.

Arrange one-third cherries and strawberries over white jelly layer, then cover with red juice and leave to set. Repeat layering until all fruit and juices have been used. Leave for 1 hour until jelly has set.

Dip mould into hand-hot water for 1-2 seconds, then invert on to a serving plate. Decorate with extra fruit or leaves and flowers.

*Serves 8.*

# FRUIT CHEESE DESSERT

| | |
|---|---|
| **60 ml (2 fl oz/¼ cup) Marsala** |
| **¼ teaspoon ground mace** |
| **185 g (6 oz/1 cup) mixed glacé fruit, chopped** |
| **375 g (12 oz/1½ cups) ricotta or cream cheese** |
| **4 teaspoons caster sugar** |
| **2 eggs, separated** |
| **2 teaspoons grated lemon peel** |
| **155 ml (5 fl oz/⅔ cup) whipping cream** |
| **fresh or glacé fruit and mint leaves, to decorate** |

Mix Marsala, mace and glacé fruit together in a bowl, stirring until well blended. Cover with plastic wrap and leave for several hours.

Put ricotta or cream cheese into a bowl, add sugar, egg yolks and lemon peel, beating with a wooden spoon until smooth. Add marinated fruit and stir until well mixed with the cheese.

Whisk egg whites; whip cream until it peaks softly. Fold alternately into cheese mixture.

Spoon into 6 small dishes and chill for 1 hour before serving. Decorate top of each dessert with fresh or glacé fruit and a mint leaf.

*Serves* 6.

# FRUIT IN WINE

155 ml (5 fl oz/⅔ cup) white wine
155 ml (5 fl oz/⅔ cup) red wine
60 g (2 oz/¼ cup) caster sugar
4 strips pared lemon peel
2 teaspoons ground mace
6 fresh lemon balm leaves
6 ripe apricots
60 g (2 oz/¼ cup) light soft brown sugar
4 cm (1½ in) cinnamon stick
4 cloves
4 strips pared orange peel
6 fresh mint leaves
6 red plums
orange and lemon twists, mint and lemon balm leaves, to decorate

Put the white and red wines into separate saucepans, each with 155 ml (5 fl oz/⅔ cup) water.

Add caster sugar, lemon peel, mace and lemon balm leaves to the white wine. Bring to the boil, add apricots, cover and cook gently 5-8 minutes or until tender.

Place the apricots carefully in a small bowl and pour over marinade so they are completely immersed. Leave until cold.

Add brown sugar, cinnamon, cloves, orange peel and mint leaves to the red wine. Bring to the boil, add plums, cover and cook very gently for 8-10 minutes, or until plums are tender.

Place the plums in a small bowl and pour over marinade to cover. Leave until cold.

Lift apricots and plums out of syrups and place on separate serving plates. Strain each marinade back into a separate saucepan and boil rapidly for 1-2 minutes, until syrupy.

Pour red syrup over plums and white syrup over apricots. When cold, decorate with orange and lemon twists, mint and lemon balm.

*Serves 3.*

# FRUIT KEBABS

| |
|---|
| **4 teaspoons dark rum or sherry** |
| **60 g (2 oz/¼ cup) caster sugar** |
| **½ fresh pineapple, flesh cut into bite-size pieces with juice reserved** |
| **2 oranges, peeled with all white pith removed and segmented with juice reserved** |
| **2 nectarines, sliced** |
| **24 cherries, stoned** |
| **2 bananas, sliced** |
| **2 teaspoons lemon juice** |
| **2 teaspoons ground cinnamon** |
| **155 ml (5 fl oz/⅔ cup) double (thick) cream** |

Mix rum and half the sugar together in a large bowl. Add pineapple and oranges with any reserved juices and nectarines and cherries.

Toss banana slices in lemon juice to prevent discoloration, then add to bowl; turn fruit in marinade to coat evenly. Cover with plastic wrap and leave for 15 minutes.

Mix together remaining sugar and cinnamon on a flat plate. Fill 6 thin wooden skewers with a mixture of fruit.

Roll each kebab in the sugar and cinnamon mixture to coat evenly. Whip cream until thick, add remaining marinade juices and fold in carefully until well blended. Place in a serving bowl.

Prepare barbecue or preheat grill. Cook kebabs for 2-3 minutes, turning once, until hot and tinged with brown. Serve with the cream.

*Serves 6.*

## MIXED FRUIT TARTS

| |
|---|
| 2 figs, sliced |
| 8 teaspoons blackcurrants |
| 90 g (3 oz) white grapes |
| 1 peach, peeled and sliced |
| 125 g (4 oz/½ cup) cream cheese |
| 155 g (5 oz/⅔ cup) natural yogurt |
| 1 teaspoon arrowroot |
| SWEET PASTRY: |
| 125 g (4 oz/1 cup) plain flour |
| 90 g (3 oz/⅓ cup) unsalted butter, chilled and diced |
| 30 g (1 oz/5 teaspoons) caster sugar |
| 1 egg yolk |
| MARINADE: |
| 8 teaspoons grenadine syrup |
| 8 teaspoons white wine or cider |
| 6 teaspoons chopped fresh apple mint |

To make pastry, put flour in a mixing bowl and rub in butter until mixture resembles breadcrumbs. Stir in sugar and egg yolk and mix to a soft dough. Wrap in plastic wrap and chill for 30 minutes.

To make marinade, mix grenadine, wine or cider and mint together in a bowl. Add fig slices, blackcurrants, grapes and peach. Turn to coat with marinade. Cover with plastic wrap and chill.

Preheat oven to 190C (375F/Gas 5). Roll out pastry thinly and line 8 individual brioche moulds or tart tins. Prick pastry with a fork and chill until firm. Bake for 8-10 minutes, until pastry is pale in colour. Cool in tin for 5 minutes, then turn out onto a wire rack.

Mix cream cheese and yogurt together. Strain marinade from fruit into a small saucepan, blend in arrowroot and bring to the boil, stirring. Cook for 30 seconds; cool.

Fill each tartlet with cream cheese mixture and fruit and glaze with marinade.

*Makes 8.*

# ROSE PETAL PAVLOVAS

| |
|---|
| 3 egg whites |
| 220 g (7 oz/1 cup) caster sugar |
| 1 teaspoon rosewater |
| 1 teaspoon raspberry vinegar |
| 1 teaspoon cornflour |
| rose pink food colouring |
| 90 g (3 oz) raspberries |
| 90 g (3 oz) strawberries, hulled and sliced |
| 125 g (4 oz) redcurrants or cherries, stoned |
| 315 ml (10 fl oz/1¼ cups) double (thick) cream |
| 125 g (4 oz/½ cup) strained Greek yogurt |
| rose petals for decoration |
| MARINADE: |
| 4 teaspoons rosewater |
| 4 teaspoons rosé wine |
| 8 teaspoons icing sugar, sifted |
| petals from 2 scented roses |

Preheat oven to 120C (250F/Gas ½). Line 2 baking sheets with baking parchment.

Whisk egg whites until stiff, then add sugar a little at a time, whisking well after each addition, until thick. Mix rosewater, vinegar, cornflour and a drop of pink food colouring together. Add to meringue and whisk until thick and glossy.

Place 12 dessertspoonfuls of meringue, spaced apart, onto baking sheet. Bake for 45 minutes. Turn off oven and leave until cold.

To make marinade, mix rosewater, rosé wine, icing sugar and rose petals together. Add fruit and turn carefully to coat evenly. Cover with plastic wrap and chill for 30 minutes.

Whip cream until thick, fold in yogurt and strain in marinade.

Arrange pavlovas on a serving plate, spoon cream onto each, top with fruit and decorate with petals.

*Makes 12.*

THE BOOK OF
# DRESSINGS & MARINADES

# INDEX

# TIPSY FRUIT CLOUD

| |
|---|
| 2 kiwi fruit, peeled and cubed |
| 2 peaches, peeled, stoned and cubed |
| ½ pineapple, peeled, cored and cubed |
| 185 g (6 oz) strawberries, hulled |
| 125 g (4 oz/½ cup) fromage frais |
| 125 ml (4 fl oz/½ cup) double (thick) cream |
| mint leaves, to decorate |
| MARINADE |
| 3 teaspoons dark rum |
| 3 teaspoons kirsch |
| 3 teaspoons peach brandy |
| 60 g (2 oz/½ cup) icing sugar, sifted |
| 2 teaspoons finely grated orange peel |

To make marinade, mix rum, kirsch, brandy, icing sugar and orange peel together in a shallow dish.

Add all fruit to marinade and turn carefully to coat evenly. Cover with plastic wrap and chill for 1-2 hours to marinate.

Whip fromage frais and cream together until thick. Strain marinade from mixed fruit into a bowl. Reserve a few pieces of fruit for decoration and carefully fold remaining fruit into cream mixture.

Divide fruit between 6 glasses and decorate with fresh mint leaves and top with reserved fruit. Serve the marinade as a sauce.

*Serves* 6.